Gifts with Meaning

HOW TO CHOOSE
UNIQUE & THOUGHTFUL PRESENTS
FOR ANY OCCASION

SHANON LYON

SASQUATCH BOOKS
SEATTLE

Printed in Canada
Published by Sasquatch Books
Distributed by PGW/Perseus
15 14 13 12 11 10 09 08   9 8 7 6 5 4 3 2 1

Cover design/illustration: Rosebud Eustace
Interior design/illustrations/composition: Rosebud Eustace

Library of Congress Cataloging-in-Publication Data
Lyon, Shanon.
 Gifts with meaning : how to choose unique and thoughtful presents for
any occasion / Shanon Lyon. -- 1st ed.
    p. cm.
 ISBN-13: 978-1-57061-566-5
 ISBN-10: 1-57061-566-7
 1. Gifts. I. Title.
 GT3040.L86 2008
 394--dc22

                          2008022778

Sasquatch Books
119 South Main Street, Suite 400
Seattle, WA 98104
(206) 467-4300
www.sasquatchbooks.com
custserv@sasquatchbooks.com

Contents

Introduction

WHAT IS A MEANINGFUL GIFT?

Every year at holiday time, my best friend gives me an ornament. It's a simple enough tradition, and for the first few years, I honestly didn't think much of it. Last Christmas, however, as I was unpacking all of our holiday decorations and setting up the tree, I was filled with joy and a feeling of closeness as I pulled her gifts from the box. There are nearly 1,500 miles between us, but that night it felt like she was right there in our living room, literally a part of our family and our celebration. As I sipped my hot chocolate, I took a moment to remember all the good times we've shared and to savor our friendship. I called her the next day to thank her. Not for the ornaments, per se—though they are lovely. What I really appreciate is her ability to create this unique vehicle of connection, a tangible way for us to remember how special our friendship is and how lucky we are.

It feels great to receive meaningful gifts from people we care about . . . but, if you're reading this book, then you know it feels even better to give them. There's nothing like knowing you picked out the perfect gift and that it came straight from the heart. There's no substitute for that unforgettable look on a loved one's face that says you've struck a chord and touched them in a way that no hastily purchased sweater or DVD could.

So what qualifies as a "meaningful gift"? Well, it depends on you, the recipient, and your relationship. I say it's any gift that's cherished and reminds the recipient that you think he or she is special. These gifts don't have to cost a lot—or anything, really—and are a great way to bring meaning into our everyday lives and connect with those around us.

Tradition can go a long way toward creating a meaningful gift. Using symbolic items can help you articulate what you can't necessarily find the words to say. Suppose you want to get your mom some flowers for Mother's Day. You plan to send a card along with them, but in pondering all the ways your mom is wonderful, you draw a blank on what to actually write. If you're aware of the symbolism of various flowers, finding the words to express how you feel—as well as deciding which flowers to actually choose—becomes a lot easier. Is your mom a one-of-a-kind picture of perfection, deserving of the camellia? Or an always-cheerful childlike spirit who might feel kinship with a buttercup?

There's also an intrinsic value in a gift that bears cultural or historical significance. Take brooms for example. They're used in wedding ceremonies all over the world and have a rich symbolic history. Giving a new couple an engraved hearth broom not only celebrates and recognizes their connection to each other, it also honors all the happy couples who've come before. Traditional gifts invite the recipients to be part of something bigger than themselves and the occasion.

Finally, and perhaps most importantly, giving a symbolic gift allows you to offer up priceless, intangible sentiments, like hope, peace, or serenity. Things are just that: things. But the

meaning behind the things you choose to give can last forever and offer the recipient something deeper and impalpable that they need, not just something they want. However, you don't want to start giving symbolic gifts willy-nilly without putting some thought into the personality of the recipient, the occasion, and the usefulness of the gift. The last thing you want is for your carefully selected gift, chock-full of tradition, to become another knick-knack on the shelf because you didn't share its meaning.

HOW DO I GET STARTED?

I know what you're thinking. This all seems a bit complicated and time consuming. And, if you're anything like me, time is a gift that you don't always have. Your circle of friends and family has grown over the years and so have your responsibilities. Get the groceries, drop the cat at the vet, take the car in for maintenance, and, oh, don't forget that your nephew's birthday is next weekend! Though we have the best intentions, more often than not we're rushed into grabbing the first thing we see.

That's where this book comes in. Consider it your guide to gifts that are meaningful, yet personal and practical. Each entry includes a traditional item (whether it's an actual object, a certain metal, an animal, etc.), an explanation of what the item symbolizes, a bit of historical background, and a few gift suggestions. The idea is to take tradition and make it relevant to you and the person you're buying for. Hats, for instance, represent a new set of responsibilities and a changed view of the world. If your sports-obsessed neighbor is heading off to college, get her a cap from her favorite team and tickets to an upcoming game. Some items have more suggestions than others as to how to incorporate them into a relevant gift. Sage or salt, for instance, are often more useful (and meaningful) when presented with accompaniments. Clocks, however, are a little more straightforward.

Even if you already have a gift in mind, this book can help you add that extra something. If your best friend's been eyeing the cashmere scarf in the Macy's window, then you know exactly what to get her. However, if she'd be happy with any color, use this book to add some significance to the scarf by choosing the color according to tradition. Do you want to wish her clarity of mind with a purple scarf or hope and peace with a green scarf? When you tell her why you chose the color, you'll elevate an already lovely gift into a truly meaningful one, and she'll be touched by the extra thought behind it (and will remember the sentiment every time she wears it).

It's important to note that this is not a comprehensive list of symbolic items or meanings. Instead, items have been chosen that best lend themselves to becoming great gifts with meanings that are most appropriate for the occasion. And though we've divided the book by occasion for ease of use, don't feel limited to a specific section. If you're looking for a gift for your husband, for instance, you might find the perfect gift under anniversaries, birthdays, or Valentine's Day.

Finally, don't forget that half the fun is to convey the background of your gift to your recipient—especially if its meaning is little-known and interesting, and will make for a

great anecdote every time they show it off. You can labor over a basket full of thoughtful, symbolic trinkets for a recently married couple, but if they don't know the meaning behind the items, they are missing out on a big part of your offering. While you may choose to simply tell the recipient the story behind a gift when giving it in person, you'll also find a section on wrapping and presenting on the following pages that will help you put the finishing touches on your gift.

And remember, when all's said and done, there is one lasting truism about any gift you give: regardless of what you choose, the gift that means the most is the one that comes from the heart.

PRESENTING YOUR GIFT

Before you deliver your gift, you may want to add a few finishing touches. These little extras are a great way to add meaning to a straight-forward gift (the video game your teenager must have) or infuse an already personal gift with even more sentiment.

WRAPPING

Whether you use wrapping paper or a nice bag and tissue, your selection should be appropriate for the person and the occasion. Add more depth by choosing a meaningful color (see Appendix C: The Meaning of Colors, pg. 131) or rubber-stamping the paper or bag with meaningful objects, like stars or pineapples.

SENTIMENTS

It's important to convey the meaning and symbolism of your gift, and the simplest way is to include it in the card: "This bamboo is a symbol of the inner strength that I admire in you. May it bring you good luck in the coming year!" Poems and sayings also work nicely. For instance, suppose you were giving a set of butterfly-embroidered pillowcases to a recently married couple. You might do a quick search for a related poem or saying and include something like this Irish blessing:

> *May the wings of the butterfly kiss the sun*
> *And find your shoulder to light on,*

> *To bring you luck, happiness, and riches*
> *Today, tomorrow, and beyond.*

ACCOUTREMENTS

Several symbolic items are easy to attach to gifts. A sprig of rosemary, representing fidelity, makes a great addition to a wedding gift, and feathers, which are thought to bring good luck and offer protection, are fitting for a variety of occasions (choose gray for good fortune, blue for health, and green for money). Here are a few other items you could easily tie on to your gift:

- A flower
- A toy airplane or automobile
- A bell
- A paper or origami animal
- A seashell
- A small bag of coins
- An ornament in a meaningful shape
- Candles
- Fresh herbs

Of course, any time you can personally deliver your gift and offer the story of the symbolism behind it in your own words, you'll convey even more meaning and the precious gift of your time.

Birthdays

Years ago, people believed they were especially vulnerable to evil spirits during times of great change, like turning a year older. To scare off any lurking demons, friends and family would gather round the person of honor and cause a stir, celebrating joyously with laughter and dancing. Gifts were thought to bring extra luck and protection.

Though we no longer battle demons on our birthdays (at least not every year), many of the traditions have remained—dancing, laughing, and the giving of gifts. A thoughtful and meaningful birthday gift says you care about the recipient and that you recognize and appreciate his or her unique personality.

Gemstones have long been thought to possess magical, healing qualities, making birthstones one of the most symbolic gifts. Aquamarine was said to calm the nerves, and emeralds helped sharpen the mind. Over time, people assigned these powerful stones to specific months and believed that those born in that month would be granted the stone's magic.

There are a variety of birthstone lists, including mystical, zodiacal, Arabic, Hebrew, and ayurvedic, but the modern list created by the American National Association of Jewelers in 1912 is the most commonly used (check out the "Birthstones" discussion in this chapter). A gift featuring a birthstone can be an excellent choice for a special birthday; however, since they can be expensive, gems may not always be in your budget. There are plenty of ways to incorporate the color of the birthstone into your gift without breaking the bank. An aquamarine umbrella, for instance, would make a great gift for the March birthday gal looking for a little extra protection against the elements.

Kids present a unique gift-giving challenge, particularly for those who want to give a meaningful or symbolic gift. When babies are born, it's easy to give a gift packed with meaning (see the New Arrivals chapter, pg. 59). But, as the bundle of joy grows from toddler to teen, it gets a little trickier. You can't expect your six-year-old nephew to appreciate the meaning behind a special book you've labored over selecting. When purchasing for kids and teens, considering packaging a small "fun" gift with something that might mean a lot more down the road. From the time I was about ten, my grandfather gave me stocks or bonds for birthdays and Christmas. At the time, I'm sure I thought the gift was predictable and maybe a little boring. But, when I wanted to gallivant around Europe as a college student, I was thrilled that my bonds had matured—and, as an adult, I appreciate the "just in case" cushion the stocks provide. I now see the value and meaning of the gift and the lessons he's shared about saving and investing, and it means a lot that he cared so much about my future.

Read on for symbols and ideas to inspire your own meaningful birthday gift giving.

AIRPLANE

Symbolizes freedom, independence, aspiration

St. Augustine said, "The world is a book, and those who do not travel read only a page." Airplanes represent an opportunity to explore and experience total freedom and independence. Similarly, flight, especially in dreams, represents achievement of one's dreams, demonstration of personal will, and liberation. This means these gifts are ideal not only for a travel lover, but anyone striving for a goal or on the verge of a new venture.

Gift Suggestions:

- **Plane tickets for a weekend getaway**
- **A model airplane**
- **Flying lessons**
- **A collection of themed movies, like *Airplane!*, *Planes, Trains and Automobiles*, and *Snakes on a Plane***

ANT

Symbolizes hard work, frugality, community, strength

A small animal with a big history, the ant is considered sacred in many cultures and a symbol of hard work and community. It can lift items many times its size and is revered in China for its order and virtue. Christians praise the frugality and preparedness of this small but mighty creature. Incorporate the ant into gifts for hardworking people or those active in their communities.

Gift Suggestions:

- ⊰ **An ant farm for a child or a kid at heart**
- ⊰ **A fancy picnic set as an ode to the ant. Fill a basket with a bottle of wine, tablecloth, cheese knife and board, napkins, silverware, and plates.**

AUTOMOBILE
Symbolizes freedom, responsibility

The car, particularly in America, is the ultimate symbol of freedom. With that freedom, especially as one embarks on adulthood, comes a responsibility to demonstrate self-control. Giving a car-themed gift is not only ideal for those turning sixteen, but for anyone setting off on their own in life.

Gift Suggestions:

- ⊰ **If the recipient has a car that he's particularly proud of, a kit with fancy car wash, wax, a chamois, and interior wipes**
- ⊰ **A car ornament or a sterling silver key chain, particularly meaningful for someone receiving her driver's license or moving to a new place**

BAMBOO
Symbolizes strength, flexibility, longevity, luck, enlightenment

Bamboo can move with the wind but not break, which makes it one of the strongest (and most flexible) building materials. Its evergreen nature is a symbol of longevity, and it's often thought to bring good luck. In Chinese philosophy, the knots on the stalk represent the various steps on the path to enlightenment. Give this gift in honor of achieving a milestone birthday, or simply because you admire the recipient's grace under pressure.

Gift Suggestions:

- A few lucky bamboo stalks in a glass jar
- A bamboo bowl filled with fruit, which is symbolic of prosperity
- A flowering plant in a bamboo box
- Towels, sheets, or pajamas made from bamboo, one of the softest fibers around

BASKET
Symbolizes abundance, fertility

Full baskets symbolize the womb and abundance. When wool or fruit is inside, they can also signify fertility. Incorporate a basket into gifts for the lady of the house or a woman who's starting a family.

Gift Suggestions:

- ⊰ For the woman who loves knitting (or would love to learn), a small basket with an assortment of cozy yarns and a knitting book
- ⊰ A basket brimming with bath items or gourmet food
- ⊰ A basket of "a few of her favorite things," with a variety of small gifts selected by friends and family members

 BATH

Symbolizes renewal, purification

Throughout history, water has been granted transformative qualities that border on magic. Baths were thought to clean both the body and the soul, simultaneously washing away dirt and sin. Bath-themed gifts are ideal for busy people who deserve a little relaxation and time for themselves.

Gift Suggestions:

- ⊰ A spa gift certificate
- ⊰ A selection of items for a relaxing bath (oils, salts, candles, music) in a small basket
- ⊰ A therapeutic footbath
- ⊰ A bathrobe and a bath sponge, loofah, or bottle of bubble bath

BIRTHSTONES

This modern birthstone list is the official list from the American National Association of Jewelers, adopted in 1912. You can find a full list of gemstone meanings and symbolism in Appendix B: The Meaning of Gemstones (pg. 129).

January	Garnet
February	Amethyst
March	Aquamarine
April	Diamond
May	Emerald
June	Pearl, Moonstone
July	Ruby
August	Peridot
September	Sapphire
October	Opal, Tourmaline
November	Citrine, Topaz
December	Turquoise, Blue Topaz

Gift Suggestions:

ᐳ **Jewelry featuring the recipient's birthstone**

ᐳ **A key chain with his birthstone and an engraved message**

BOOK
Symbolizes knowledge, wisdom

Books are a bottomless well of knowledge and wisdom and often a symbol of high culture. In a sense, they represent the universe and all it holds. Give the gift of knowledge to anyone embarking on a new phase in life or to someone whose wisdom you cherish.

Gift Suggestions:

- ⊰ A first edition or signed copy of his favorite book
- ⊰ A beautiful blank book to record her own wisdom and inner thoughts
- ⊰ A copy of your favorite book, and an invitation to discuss it over dinner
- ⊰ The first volume of a book collection on a certain topic or genre, with plans to add to it every year

CEDAR
Symbolizes strength, support, protection, calm

Prized for its strength and its resistance to rot, cedar was used to build Solomon's Temple in Jerusalem. Origen, an early church father, said, "The cedar does not decay. To use cedar for the beams of our house is to protect our soul from corruption." It's used in aromatherapy to ease anxiety and fear. Cedar gifts are a way to show support or to thank others for theirs.

Gift Suggestions:

- ❧ A set of cedar hangers
- ❧ A new sweater or blanket and a cedar sachet to store with it
- ❧ A cedar box or chest for treasures
- ❧ Cedar essential oil and a diffuser
- ❧ A cedar plank for the home chef, along with a grilling cookbook

CHERRY

Symbolizes spring, beauty, youth, protection, femininity

From blossom to fruit, the cherry holds many meanings. In Japan, the blossom represents spring, beauty, youth, and femininity. And in ancient China, the wood of the cherry tree was thought to ward off evil spirits. Cherry-themed gifts are ideal for young women and the young at heart; they also make a lovely choice for spring birthdays.

Gift Suggestions:

- ❧ A cherry blossom sprig in a bud vase
- ❧ Homemade cherry jam or pie
- ❧ A selection of cherry-scented lotion, bubble bath, or candles
- ❧ A small jar of fresh or brandied cherries, with a recipe card on how to use them

CHEST

Symbolizes treasure, revelation, heart

Chests, or coffers, hold treasure to be revealed at a later date. Containers like this are also often associated with the heart. Famous coffers include the Ark of the Covenant, which held the Ten Commandments, and Pandora's box, keeper of hope. Chest-themed gifts can be straightforward, like a jewelry box, or more abstract, like a sealed letter to be opened on a certain date in the future. The delayed gift is ideal for people making big changes in their lives. Opening the "chest" can be a moment of great revelation, and the contents a testament to how far they've come.

Gift Suggestions:

- **A set of stationery. Ask her to write a letter to herself about her hopes and dreams for the future. Put the letter in an envelope, seal it, and send it to her on her next birthday.**
- **A time capsule. Include favorite magazines, stubs from events, letters or postcards, and pictures. Seal it up and give it as a gift that can't be opened until his next big birthday.**
- **A small box or chest with a special note or meaningful touchstone inside**
- **A jewelry box with a special piece of jewelry**

COMPASS
Symbolizes direction, balance, spiritual journey

The compass symbolizes direction or finding one's way and makes a great gift for anyone on a journey. In Chinese tradition, the feng shui compass, or Lo P'an, is used to provide deeper meaning about all physical and energetic aspects of a location.

Gift Suggestions:

- ↲ **A compass plus a guidebook to somewhere he's been longing to go (figuratively or literally)**
- ↲ **A compass and a subscription to a travel magazine**
- ↲ **A compass with driving gloves and a selection of maps**

 ## EARRINGS
Symbolize nobility, power, authority

Since ears were pierced in many civilizations, long earlobes (possibly stretched by earrings) symbolized nobility, authority, and power.

Gift Suggestions:

- ↲ **A pair of earrings featuring the recipient's birthstone**
- ↲ **A pair of homemade earrings or earrings from a local jeweler**

ELEPHANT
Symbolizes good luck, wisdom, strength

Elephants are symbols of good fortune in feng shui and valued in Asia for their wisdom and strength, which makes them a meaningful symbol for students of all kinds. Some believe that the trunk of the elephant must turn upward in order for it to bring good luck.

Gift Suggestions:

- **Zoos house hundreds of symbolic animals. Surprise him with a trip to the zoo and be surrounded by wisdom, good luck, and strength.**
- **An elephant adopted in her name**
- **An elephant-shaped figurine, card, ornament, or pendant**

FIG
Symbolizes enlightenment, peace, abundance

It was under the fig tree that Siddhartha Gautama (the Buddha) reached enlightenment, and, in the Bible, a fig-bearing tree is thought to be a symbol of paradise. The fig makes a great gift for anyone in search of peace and a sense of well-being.

Gift Suggestions:

- **A basket of fresh figs or fig jam**
- **A potted fig tree**
- **Fig-scented candles, soap, or bath oil**

◄ **A dinner made by you featuring figs and other meaning-ful foods, like pomegranates, which symbolize prosperity**

FLOWERS

Flowers are rich in symbolism. You can find a detailed list of flowers and their meanings in Appendix A: The Meaning of Flowers & Trees (pg. 125). Traditional birth flowers are listed below.

January	Carnation
February	Iris
March	Daffodil
April	Daisy
May	Lily of the Valley
June	Rose
July	Larkspur
August	Gladiola
September	Aster
October	Marigold
November	Chrysanthemum
December	Paperwhite Narcissus

FOUR-LEAF CLOVER
Symbolizes hope, faith, love, luck

A typical three-leaf clover is said to represent the trinity, but a classic good luck charm, the four-leaf clover, represents hope, faith, love, and most of all, luck.

Gift Suggestions:

- ☸ **A four-leaf clover inside an invitation to spend a day at the park (and perhaps find more good luck!)**
- ☸ **A four-leaf clover charm, pin, pendant, or card, especially for someone embarking on a new venture**

HAT
Symbolizes status, responsibility, new beginnings

You can often tell a person's occupation or status just by glancing at his hat (baker, king, graduate), and people who "wear many hats" have numerous responsibilities and jobs. A new hat can welcome a new phase of life and encourage new ways of thinking, which makes it perfect for those celebrating a milestone birthday.

Gift Suggestions:

- ☸ **A hat from a favorite sporting team and tickets to the game**
- ☸ **Everything needed to knit a hat and instructions on how to do so**

◁ **A new hat appropriate for the season (sun hat, ski hat, cozy hat, gardening hat)**

LADDER
Symbolizes upward movement, enlightenment

Ladders symbolize moving from one place to another, often up toward heaven or enlightenment. Pictures of ladders were even placed inside Egyptian tombs, perhaps to help the dead get where they were going. Ladder symbolism is perfect for your favorite corporate climber or anyone moving upward in life.

Gift Suggestions:

◁ **A gift certificate to a home improvement store for a ladder or whatever else will help the recipient accomplish his goals**

◁ **A gift certificate for a night in a tree house (there are tree house resorts in several states)**

LIGHTBULB
Symbolizes spirit, ideas

Generally, light represents the spirit, and lightbulbs are often used in cartoons and pop culture to signify a brilliant idea. Give these gifts to the creative person who might appreciate a little extra juice.

Gift Suggestions:

- ⊰ **A package of energy-saving light bulbs and a book on going green for your eco-minded pal**

- ⊰ **A lightbulb and a coffee-table book on amazing inventions to spark big ideas for an aspiring entrepreneur**

- ⊰ **An interesting new lamp or reading light for the bookworm**

 LOTUS

Symbolizes new beginnings, enlightenment, strength, purity, art

The lotus is associated with the creation of the world, blossoming from the dark beginnings of the universe. In India, it's a revered symbol for spirituality and art. The lotus embodies strength, purity, and enlightenment of the human soul and makes a symbolic gift for those whose quiet strength you admire.

Gift Suggestions:

- ⊰ **A piece of clothing featuring an image of a lotus and a gift certificate to a yoga class**

- ⊰ **A trip to a local botanical garden (present the gift with a lotus flower and a card)**

- ⊰ **A nice teapot and a tin of tea containing lotus flower (like Orange and Lotus Flower Green Tea)**

- ⊰ **A lotus bamboo plant**

MAKEUP
Symbolizes protection

In ancient Egypt, makeup was applied to protect the wearer from evil. Lipstick was worn to keep evil spirits from entering through the mouth and to prevent the woman's soul from escaping.

Gift Suggestions:

- ⊰ **A tube of lip gloss and a gift certificate to a makeup store, like Sephora or Aveda**
- ⊰ **A facial or makeover at a spa**
- ⊰ **A lovely new makeup case for travel**
- ⊰ **A beautiful engraved compact, makeup mirror, or lipstick case**

MAZE
Symbolizes discovery, self-awareness, meditation, revelation

Mazes represent the unique journey to one's true self and the epiphanies and lessons that come from life's more trying times. Psychologists believe that the paths of the maze represent confusion; when you find the center, you've discovered your authentic self. Walking labyrinths is also a form of meditation. If you know someone who's doing some inner searching, a maze-themed gift is sure to be appreciated.

Gift Suggestions:

- A weekend retreat to a place with a labyrinth
- A big book of mazes and puzzles and a box of sharp pencils
- A small toy maze for his desk

 RABBIT
Symbolizes luck, art, intelligence, fertility

In Chinese astrology, the rabbit represents intelligence, luck, and artistic ability. Rabbits also multiply quickly, which makes them a popular symbol of fertility. In American folklore, rabbit's feet are considered good luck charms. Rabbit-themed gifts are appropriate for creative types and anyone in need of a little luck.

Gift Suggestions:

- An illustrated copy of *Alice's Adventures in Wonderland*, by Lewis Carroll, or *The Velveteen Rabbit*, by Margery Williams, classics suitable for adults and kids
- A set of colored pencils and a sketchbook to help her get in touch with her inner artist
- The Rabbit corkscrew and French Rabbit wine
- A stuffed bunny or rabbit's foot

STAR
Symbolizes honor, hope, order

A bright spot in the dark night, stars are a symbol of hope and, in the United States, of sovereignty and honor. Due to their constant placement in the night sky, they're seen as a sign of cosmic order. Star-themed gifts are perfect for the people who always brighten your day and are a source of light and joy.

Gift Suggestions:

- A telescope and a book on constellations
- A star-shaped ornament, figurine, or pendant
- A star-shaped candle
- A map of the night sky on the day of his birth

 THREAD
Symbolizes connection, devotion

Thread is one of the oldest symbols, representing the connection between different worlds. Priestly Hindus wear a sacred thread in a loop around the left shoulder and under the right arm; the thread symbolizes ancient rituals and serves as a reminder of the wearer's duties and commitments. These make great gifts for someone who's miles away but to whom you feel eternally connected.

Gift Suggestions:

- An embroidered tea towel or scarf
- A monogrammed towel or robe

᙮ For someone who sews, a basket of beautifully colored spools of thread and/or embroidery floss, plus a book of patterns

UMBRELLA
Symbolizes dignity, honor, protection

Also known as parasols, umbrellas represent dignity and honor and are often associated with royalty. They protect people from sun and rain and are said by some to symbolize the celestial sphere. Give an umbrella to someone who you honor or put on a pedestal, or to anyone in need of a little protection against the elements.

Gift Suggestions:

᙮ A fancy umbrella and a list or book of things to do on a rainy day

᙮ A whimsical umbrella with matching rain boots, rain hat, or slicker

CHILDREN'S BIRTHDAYS

Here are a few ways to customize these gifts for children.

BOOK
Symbolizes knowledge, wisdom

Books are a bottomless well of knowledge and wisdom and often a symbol of high culture. In a sense, they represent the universe and all it holds.

Gift Suggestions:

- A collection of your favorite books from childhood
- A blank book or diary for him or her to fill in
- A blank book in which you write your own story for the birthday child, starring him or her. You can draw your own pictures or use clippings from magazines.

CARP
Symbolizes strength, patience, determination

Because it swims upstream, the carp is a symbol for persistence and determination in Japan. On Children's Day in May, carp-shaped streamers are flown to celebrate all members of the family.

Gift Suggestions:

- A day spent fishing with you
- A jar of gummy or candy fish

COINS
Symbolize wealth, luck, prosperity

In Britain, lucky sixpences are given for many occasions, including birthdays. Silver also promotes wholeness and harbors a calming energy.

Gift Suggestions:

- ⊰ **A piggy bank and a CD or bond**
- ⊰ **An automatic coin sorter (and a few coins to go inside it)**
- ⊰ **A coin purse (ditto)**
- ⊰ **A coin-collecting book or kit**
- ⊰ **A special coin from his or her birth year**

MONKEY
Symbolizes disciplined mind, health, success

Smart and cheerful, monkeys symbolize a disciplined mind, health, and success. The proverb "See no evil, hear no evil, and speak no evil" came from Japan's Three Wise Monkeys, an image of three monkeys who symbolize this principle.

Gift Suggestions:

- ⊰ **A selection of monkey-themed games or books**
- ⊰ **All the materials to make a sock monkey and a how-to book**

↛ **A stuffed monkey and a certificate good for a trip to the zoo with you**

UNICORN
Symbolizes purity, wisdom, longevity, strength

Long a part of fantasy and dreams, unicorns generally symbolize goodness, strength, and purity. In China specifically, they represent wisdom and longevity. According to folklore, the unicorn's horn could counteract poison, and this mythical creature could only be caught by a virgin.

Gift Suggestions:

↛ **A unicorn figurine, holiday ornament, or pendant**

↛ **A copy of *The Last Unicorn*, by Peter S. Beagle (suitable for older children)**

↛ **A shirt or pajamas featuring the unicorn**

Weddings & Wedding Showers

Nearly every moment of a traditional wedding ceremony bears some type of historical significance or symbolism, from the garter to the wedding bands to the veil. Though these traditions and rituals vary from culture to culture, the underlying message is the same: hope for a happy, fertile life free from evil.

The white wedding dress is a symbol of purity. The wedding bands are a symbol of faithfulness. And the joint cutting of the cake represents the couple's first task together and the beginning of a shared life. So where do all the toaster ovens and towels fit in? The tradition of giving gifts may have originated with dowries, gifts or money given by the groom to the bride's family for her hand in marriage or by the bride's family to the groom as an enticement to marry. These gifts included everything from cows and goats to blankets or beer. It was also not uncommon for the bride and groom's families to exchange gifts or for the mother-in-law to give a gift to the new bride to welcome her into the family.

Finnish brides typically went door-to-door with a pillowcase and collected gifts. An older married man would escort her and shelter her with an umbrella. In Scotland, the bride's mother holds a "showing of presents" a few weeks before the wedding. Gifts are unwrapped (and assembled if necessary) and displayed with the name of the giver. Friends and family come to the home, open-house style, and mingle with other guests and members of the bridal party.

Regardless of the origination of the traditions or the rituals surrounding them, giving a wedding gift is a way to express sincere wishes of happiness and prosperity for the new couple.

If you're married, you probably have gifts that you still cherish fondly and others that you don't treasure quite as much, like that lawn ornament from your great aunt Edith. Before you choose your gift, take some time to reflect on both parties, their personalities, their needs, and their likes and dislikes. Young couples, for instance, might need a variety of basic household goods, whereas an older couple may already have plenty of silverware. According to etiquette maven Emily Post, while you should ideally send your gift to the bride before the wedding or to the couple shortly thereafter, sending a gift within three months is still tasteful, so take your time!

Today, many couples register for household items at department or specialty stores, thanks to Marshall Field's, the Chicago store that launched the concept in 1924. Buying from a gift registry might seem uninspired, but it is a practical way to make sure the bride and groom get the things they need. After all, unique and meaningful gifts are nice, but they won't toast a slice of bread or serve up a nice glass of cabernet. Consider incorporating items on the registry with something more symbolic. Let's say the new couple has a set of knives on their registry. You can buy the knives and include a gift certificate to a local fish market or restaurant to symbolize fertility. Or, purchase the knives and tie a sprig of rosemary on the gift to represent fidelity. And, again, don't forget to include the symbolism of the item in your card. In a ceremony filled with so many traditions, it's easy for meaning to get lost in the mix.

ALMOND
Symbolizes good luck, fertility, prosperity, happiness

In France, almonds are a symbol of a happy marriage. Dragées, which are sugar-covered almonds, are a French delicacy and date back as far as the Roman Empire. They accompany most French ceremonies and are known as Jordan almonds in the United States and "confetti" in Italy.

Gift Suggestions:

- A coffee grinder, bag of gourmet beans, and almond syrup
- A beautiful candy dish and a jar of dragées
- A cake platter and a recipe for almond cake

AMBER
Symbolizes protection, fertility, fidelity, eternal love

In Latvia, rings of amber were used as wedding bands, and in Rome, it was worn to enhance fertility. Sometimes referred to as "solidified sunshine," amber was said to have magical healing qualities and the ability to protect the wearer against the evil eye.

Gift Suggestions:

- ⊰ **A chess set made from amber**
- ⊰ **An amber glass bowl or serving platter**
- ⊰ **An amber glass decanter and bottle of wine**
- ⊰ **Perfume or a set of essential oils in amber glass bottles**
- ⊰ **Amber essential oil and a diffuser**

BASKET
Symbolizes fertility, wholeness, abundance

When a basket is full, it's said to represent abundance, fruition, and fertility. In ancient Egypt, baskets symbolized wholeness and togetherness. And in the Cahuilla Native American tradition, baskets were often given as gifts, symbolizing great wealth. A basket is a great way to package other meaningful gifts.

Gift Suggestions:

- ⊰ **A basket with fruit, which represents prosperity and fertility, or other gourmet treats**
- ⊰ **If the new couple has a fireplace, a basket with wood to represent new beginnings and warmth**
- ⊰ **A pretty picnic or all-purpose basket filled with small miscellaneous items from the registry**

BEAN

Symbolizes beginnings, growth

Beans are seedlings to new plants and therefore symbolize great beginnings and growth.

Gift Suggestions:

- ⊰ Nine-bean soup mix with a tureen and/or a set of soup bowls
- ⊰ A set of gardening tools, a gardening book or subscription to a gardening magazine, and a package of green bean seeds
- ⊰ A pound of coffee beans and a subscription to a coffee-of-the-month club

BELL

Symbolizes presence, harmony, listening

Bells symbolize connection, wisdom, awareness, and listening. What better way to christen a new marriage than with hopes for open hearts, open minds, and, most importantly, open ears? A bell-themed gift is a lovely way to remind the couple to always be present with each other, hear each other out, and live in harmony.

Gift Suggestions:

- ⊰ An antique dinner bell
- ⊰ A collection of holiday CDs featuring bells

- ❧ Two bells, one from the groom's home state or country and one from the bride's. Tie with a white bow to symbolize the joining of the couple.

- ❧ The movie *It's a Wonderful Life* (featuring the line "Every time a bell rings, an angel gets its wings") and an engraved bell ornament

- ❧ A collector's edition of *Peter Pan*, featuring the one and only Tinker Bell

BROOM

Symbolizes purity, cleanliness, protection

Brooms have a long history of cultural significance, sweeping away the old to make room for the new. In ancient shrines, sweeping was an act of worship, and in African-American tradition, the bride and groom jumped over a broomstick at the end of a wedding ceremony. Whoever jumped the highest was the decision maker of the household.

Gift Suggestions:

- ❧ A handcrafted or personalized broom along with a gift certificate for a cleaning service

- ❧ A woven basket with a broom, dustpan, and various organic cleaning supplies

- ❧ A personalized hearth broom

BUTTERFLY
Symbolizes marital happiness, new beginnings

Caterpillars cocoon and turn into beautiful butterflies, representing rebirth and new beginnings. In the East, two butterflies together are a symbol of love and a happy marriage.

Gift Suggestions:

- Thank-you notes with two butterflies on the front (store-bought or homemade using card stock and rubber stamps)
- A selection of household items decorated with butterflies: candles, dessert plates, kitchen towels, or napkin rings

COINS
Symbolize support, prosperity, protection

In Mexican wedding ceremonies, the groom presents the bride with thirteen coins and promises to support her throughout their marriage. In many cultures, silver is thought to ward off evil. Some brides place a lucky sixpence in their shoe to bring good luck and wealth to their marriages.

Gift Suggestions:

- A silver piggy bank along with a check to get them started
- Commemorative coins from the year of their births plus the year of their union

COPPER MOLDS

Symbolize love, wealth

According to folklore, if a couple hangs copper molds in the kitchen, they'll not only bring love vibrations to the room, they'll also attract money to the household.

Gift Suggestions:

- ⌁ A copper cupcake mold with a cupcake cookbook and decorating set
- ⌁ Decorative copper molds for hanging in the kitchen
- ⌁ A baking-themed gift basket including copper molds as well as gourmet mixes and embellishments

CRYSTAL

Symbolizes earth, purity, clarity

Crystals are thought to have magical powers and represent the earth element in Chinese feng shui. Crystal symbolizes purity and clarity.

Gift Suggestions:

- ⌁ A crystal vase tied with a red ribbon (the symbol for romance in feng shui). (The vase should be placed in the southwest corner of the couple's bedroom for a harmonious and happy marriage.)

⊰ A gift certificate for a trip to a fortune-teller for a look inside a crystal ball

⊰ A set of crystal wine or champagne glasses

⊰ An engraved crystal bowl or decanter

DOVE

Symbolizes peace, purity, love

In the Bible, a dove was sent from the ark and it came back carrying an olive branch. Since then, doves have been seen as a sign of peace and a symbol of innocence and love. Two doves together are often seen as a symbol of marital bliss.

Gift Suggestions:

⊰ A glass candy dish and a selection of Dove chocolates

⊰ A dove holiday ornament engraved with the newlyweds' names and wedding date

EGG

Symbolizes fertility, rebirth, hope

One of the most ancient symbols, the egg, for obvious reasons, is seen as a symbol of fertility and new life. It represents both the womb and the universe.

Gift Suggestions:

⊰ A decorative egg

ᴗ An "egg hunt" for the new couple: Fill plastic eggs with mini surprises, including gift certificates for a spa treatment for two, dinner, or an overnight stay at a bed-and-breakfast, and tuck them into a basket.

ᴗ An engraved egg holiday ornament

ELEPHANT

Symbolizes wisdom, good luck, strength

The elephant-headed Ganesha is an important deity in the Hindu tradition, and elephants are often featured in Indian weddings. Elephants are also symbols of good fortune in feng shui and valued in Asia for their intelligence. Some believe that the trunk of the elephant must turn upward in order for it to bring good luck.

Gift Suggestions:

ᴗ A membership to the zoo in the couple's town

ᴗ Two elephants adopted in the couple's names

ᴗ An elephant figurine or ornament for the home

FISH

Symbolizes fertility, prosperity

In many cultures, fish are associated with fertility, perhaps because they produce so many eggs at once. In China, the goldfish symbolizes an abundance of gold.

Gift Suggestions:

- A gift certificate to a nearby seafood restaurant (or a restaurant for them to try on their honeymoon)
- A romantic seafood dinner at their place prepared (and cleaned up) by you
- A goldfish in a pretty bowl or small aquarium
- A beautiful fish platter
- Membership to the local aquarium

FLAME
Symbolizes the soul, love, purification

The soul of the marriage is often referred to as a flame, as in "keeping the flame alive." In fact, in Italy, diamonds in engagement rings were said to be created by the "flames of love." In South Africa, the couple's parents would carry a fire from their own homes to the newlyweds' hearth.

Gift Suggestions:

- A set of hearth tools
- Candlesticks and a set of candles
- A glassblowing class for two

THE FRUITS OF MARRIAGE

Fruits are full of symbolism, and many are fitting for a meaningful wedding gift.

APPLE
Symbolizes love, fertility

Although in the Bible the apple represents temptation, it also symbolizes love and fertility. One of the first fruits harvested by man, it's an emblem of Venus and, according to myth, was created by Dionysus, the god of intoxication.

FIG
Symbolizes enlightenment, fertility, peace, abundance

It was under the fig tree that Siddhartha Gautama (the Buddha) reached enlightenment, and, in the Bible, a fig-bearing tree represents paradise. In Rome the fig is thought to symbolize fertility, and in Bulgaria figs are often thrown at newly married couples instead of rice. The many seeds represent abundance and prosperity.

LEMON
Symbolizes heart, purity, cleanliness

Lemons are thought to represent purity and cleanliness, and in Judaism, this tart fruit is a symbol of the human heart.

ORANGE
Symbolizes good fortune, fertility

Due to the number of seeds, oranges symbolize both good fortune and fertility.

PEACH
Symbolizes protection, fertility

The peach tree blossoms early in China, and so is said to symbolize fertility. The wood of the tree is thought to ward off evil spirits.

PLUM
Symbolizes sexuality, fidelity

In Christianity, the plum represents fidelity and, in dream interpretation, it's sometimes considered a symbol of female sexuality.

POMEGRANATE
Symbolizes prosperity, fertility

In China, family members exchanged pomegranate blossoms as a symbol of prosperity and to encourage the birth of sons. Pomegranate juice was also used in Rome to cure infertility.

Gift Suggestions:

- A small basket of essential oils and scented candles, and/or fresh fruits
- A fruit tree (or a gift certificate for one from a nursery) for the couple's backyard
- A subscription to a fruit-of-the-month club
- A basket of symbolic fruits and a note on what each one symbolizes
- A basket with fruit-scented lotions, candles, and bubble bath

GARLIC
Symbolizes protection, fertility

A classic symbol, garlic protects against evil. In China, this potent bulb is also considered lucky and thought to bless couples with many children.

Gift Suggestion:

- ⊰ **A garlic press, a garlic braid, and a garlic cookbook**

GOBLET
Symbolizes faithfulness, love

In Christian weddings, a bride and groom may use a special set of goblets or glasses for the traditional toast. In Japanese weddings, the couple exchanges thimble-sized cups of sake as a symbol of fidelity. In Wiccan tradition, a procreation ritual is performed with a chalice (representing female) and a ceremonial knife (representing male).

Gift Suggestions:

- ⊰ **A set of wine goblets and a bottle of wine or liqueur to be opened on a future anniversary**
- ⊰ **A bottle of bubbly and two champagne glasses—different from the rest of their glassware registry—to be used only for intimate celebrations *à deux***
- ⊰ **Two goblets engraved with their wedding date**

HAZELNUT
Symbolizes fertility, luck

The hazelnut has been said to cure common colds and baldness and to provide clairvoyance. In Celtic cultures, the nut represents fertility, symbolizing a fruitful marriage, and people were said to have strung hazelnuts on a cord and hung them in their rooms to bring good fortune.

Gift Suggestions:

- A hazelnut tree for the couple's yard (or a nursery gift certificate for one)
- A gourmet gift basket featuring flavored hazelnuts
- A silver nutcracker with a decorative jar of hazelnuts
- A hazelnut-scented candle along with a gift certificate to a home store

 ## HONEY
Symbolizes fertility, sweetness

Honey represents fertility, preservation, and sweetness and is often referred to as "heavenly dew." The term "honeymoon" comes from the idea that the first month of marriage is sweet.

Gift Suggestions:

- A gift of honeybees (in the couple's names) to an underdeveloped country through Heifer International

- A gift box of gourmet honeys and crumpets or other treats
- A glass jar decorated as if it were a brand of gourmet honey. Fill the jar with cash for the couple to spend on a "sweet" honeymoon. Tie a gold ribbon around the lid.
- Honey-scented candles, soaps, and bath items for a romantic spa evening

HORSESHOE

Symbolizes good luck, protection, fertility

A well-known symbol of good luck, the horseshoe is also a symbol of fertility and is hung on doors to protect the home from evil.

Gift Suggestions:

- A horseshoe door knocker
- An engraved horseshoe with the family name and the date of the wedding

JASMINE

Symbolizes love, happiness

This fragrant flower is the Hindu symbol for love and was often carried in bridal bouquets. In Christianity, it represents happiness.

Gift Suggestions:

- A set of sheets from the registry and jasmine-scented linen spray
- A tea set for two and jasmine tea

KNOT
Symbolizes love, matrimony, unity

The knot has a long history in weddings, from ancient Rome when a bride's girdle was secured with a knot to Hindu tradition where the garments of the couple are tied together. Knots represent the binding quality of love, hence the phrase "to tie the knot."

Gift Suggestions:

- Matching Celtic knot key chains
- A hammock big enough for two
- A few camping supplies (for the outdoorsy couple) and a book on tying knots
- A gift certificate for a double rock-climbing lesson at an indoor gym

MIRROR
Symbolizes harmony, happy marriage

You've heard that breaking a mirror garners you seven years of bad luck, but in ancient China, the mirror was a symbol of marital happiness and was said to protect the bride from evil influences.

Gift Suggestion:

  ৰ **A decorative mirror for the home**

MORTAR AND PESTLE
Symbolizes creation, unity

The mortar and pestle represent female and male, and together they symbolize creation and change.

Gift Suggestion:

  ৰ **A marble mortar and pestle alongside a Thai or Indian cookbook**

RICE
Symbolizes fertility, possibility

A life-giving seed often thrown at wedding ceremonies, rice represents fertility and possibility.

Gift Suggestion:

  ৰ **A rice cooker and a big bag of jasmine rice (jasmine is a symbol of love)**

ROSEMARY
Symbolizes fidelity, remembrance

During the Middle Ages, this fragrant herb was often used in the bride's bouquet or given to the guests as favors. Other folklore claimed that if a bride put dried rosemary in the bedsheets

or under her pillow, her groom would remain faithful. In the Czech Republic, it was once a tradition for the bride's friends to present her with a rosemary crown to represent loyalty and remembrance.

Gift Suggestions:

- ⋇ A collection of dried herbs in a spice rack
- ⋇ Rosemary-scented room spray, sachets, and candles
- ⋇ A potted rosemary plant for the home or yard
- ⋇ A sprig of rosemary tied to a gift from the registry
- ⋇ A roasting pan, a roasted chicken recipe card, and fresh or dried rosemary

 SHELL

Symbolizes wealth, female energy, fertility

In China, a shell represents wealth and a blissful journey. Many shells, particularly mollusks, symbolize female energy and fertility.

Gift Suggestions:

- ⋇ Fresh pasta shells, homemade or gourmet sauce, and a bottle of wine
- ⋇ A gift certificate for a weekend getaway to a beach resort, wrapped in a box with a seashell

SUGAR

Symbolizes luck, sweetness

In traditional Greek weddings, the bride often placed a lump of sugar in her wedding glove to ensure a sweet life.

Gift Suggestions:

- An antique sugar bowl or one that matches their dinnerware registry
- Sugar cookie mix, a few baking sheets, and personalized pot holders

 ## TURTLE

Symbolizes fertility, domesticity, determination, strength

Because turtles produce so many eggs, they're seen in many cultures as a symbol of fertility and domesticity. Psychologists see turtles as a symbol of quiet strength, and in Aesop's fable *The Tortoise and the Hare*, the turtle represents steadfastness and tenacity.

Gift Suggestions:

- A stone turtle for the couple's garden
- A ceramic turtle doorstop
- Snorkeling gear for their honeymoon

VASE
Symbolizes treasure, miracle, unity

Before Native American wedding ceremonies, the couple drinks simultaneously from a wedding vase with two spouts to symbolize their union. After the ceremony, the vase is treasured and protected for the duration of the marriage.

Gift Suggestion:

⊰ **A beautiful vase for the home**

 ## WHEAT SHEAF
Symbolizes fertility, abundance

Long used to represent the fertility of the soil, the wheat sheaf symbolizes abundance and growth.

Gift Suggestion:

⊰ **A lavender and wheat sheaf bouquet that can be dried and hung in the couple's home**

 ## WOOD
Symbolizes fertility, luck

As a symbol of fertility and luck, in Holland and Switzerland pine trees were often planted outside a couple's new home. Wood guards against hunger and evil, represents new beginnings, and helps to feed the fire in the hearth, which is the heart of the home.

Gift Suggestions:

- ⸭ A tree for the couple's yard or wooden planter boxes
- ⸭ A wooden bowl, platter, or breakfast-in-bed trays
- ⸭ A set of classic wooden games, like chess and backgammon
- ⸭ A bundle of wood and a log rack or basket

Anniversaries

Each wedding anniversary is a triumph. And whether you're looking for a gift for your spouse or your parents, it's an occasion steeped in tradition. Assigning specific materials to anniversary years likely began in medieval Germany when friends presented couples with silver wreaths on their twenty-fifth anniversary and gold wreaths on their fiftieth.

The silver and gold anniversaries were joined by a few other materials in Emily Post's *Etiquette in Society, in Business, in Politics, and at Home* in 1922. And in 1937, the American National Retail Jewelers Association published a full list of traditional anniversary gifts. Years later, a modern list was developed. It's fairly similar to the traditional list with the exception of a few "easy" or straightforward gifts here and there (like appliances or desk sets). Because of its history and deeper meaning, the traditional list features in this book.

The list of prescribed gifts starts simply (and affordably) with paper. As the anniversaries progress, so does the value (and the price). If cost is a concern, consider having family members and friends go in on a gift for special anniversaries, like the twenty-fifth or fiftieth.

Abiding by the traditional list does require a bit of creativity—though according to Post, it's not necessary to follow the list exactly. Try to think about the materials in a variety of ways. What color is the material? Are there alternate meanings of the word? The fortieth anniversary is ruby, but your gift doesn't have to be an actual ruby. What about ruby red sheets for the lovebirds? Or a gift certificate to a local restaurant with "ruby" in the name? A gorgeous red glass vase? If you know exactly what you want to get your friends for their seventh anniversary (and it has nothing to do with wool or copper), don't fret. Buy that perfect gift, wrap it in copper wrapping paper and tie it up with some wool yarn.

YEAR: 1

Tradition: Paper

Gift Suggestions:

- A pair of concert tickets
- A set of personalized stationery
- A book of IOU coupons for dinner, massage, chores, etc.
- A nice journal or sketchbook
- A first edition or signed copy of a favorite book
- An origami kit
- A love note
- An ad in the newspaper wishing the couple a happy anniversary
- A collection of your first year of correspondence
- A picnic in the park (with paper plates, of course)

YEAR: 2
Tradition: Cotton

Gift Suggestions:

- ⋈ A set of organic cotton sheets
- ⋈ A set of matching robes or slippers and a spa gift certificate for massages
- ⋈ A cotton hammock big enough for two
- ⋈ A handmade cotton quilt
- ⋈ A jazz CD as an ode to Harlem's Cotton Club
- ⋈ A romantic weekend getaway to one of the seventeen cotton-producing states, like Georgia or California

YEAR: 3
Tradition: Leather

Gift Suggestions:

- ⋈ A new piece of luggage and a surprise getaway
- ⋈ A special photo in a leather frame
- ⋈ A leather-bound book or journal
- ⋈ A leather wallet or purse with a gift card inside
- ⋈ A pair of cowboy boots (or a hat) and an afternoon of horseback riding
- ⋈ For the football fan, a new football and tickets to a special game

YEAR: 4
Tradition: Fruits/Flowers

Gift Suggestions:

- ⊰ A subscription to a flower- or fruit-of-the-month club
- ⊰ A flowering or fruit tree for the yard
- ⊰ A bouquet of flowers
- ⊰ A surprise getaway to Napa Valley or other scenic fruit-producing region

YEAR: 5
Tradition: Wood

Gift Suggestions:

- ⊰ A classic wooden game, like chess or backgammon
- ⊰ A nice bottle of wine in an engraved wooden box
- ⊰ A bundle of firewood and an invitation to a romantic evening by the fire
- ⊰ A tree for the couple's yard
- ⊰ A personalized welcome sign for the couple's home
- ⊰ A selection of woodsy massage oils, like cedarwood, sandalwood, frankincense, or eucalyptus, and a book on massage
- ⊰ A picnic or sunset walk in the woods

YEAR: 6
Tradition: Iron/Candy

Gift Suggestions:

- A collection of candy jewelry, like Ring Pops and candy necklaces, along with one piece of real jewelry
- A trip to a local amusement park for some cotton candy and a few spins on the carousel
- A gift box of gourmet candy or a year's supply of the couple's favorite sweet treat
- A weekend getaway to Hershey, Pennsylvania
- A gym membership for the couple to "pump some iron"
- Cast-iron cookware or hearth tools

YEAR: 7
Tradition: Wool/Copper

Gift Suggestions:

- Hand-knitted wool scarves, hats, or gloves
- A wool blanket or throw
- A trip that incorporates the symbols; for example, Ireland to see sheep or Copper Mountain ski resort in Colorado (wear your wool hats!)
- A copper kettle and a selection of teas and gourmet hot chocolates
- Copper wind chimes

YEAR: 8
Tradition: Bronze

Gift Suggestions:

- ⊰ A bronze fountain or birdbath for the yard
- ⊰ A bronze bottle opener and a bottle of wine
- ⊰ A tropical getaway with plenty of time to lie by the pool and get bronzed
- ⊰ A bronze sculpture (go all out and commission a sculpture of the couple!)
- ⊰ A bronzed piece of memorabilia from the couple's wedding (favor, garter, etc.)
- ⊰ An antique bronze bell

YEAR: 9
Tradition: Pottery

Gift Suggestions:

- ⊰ A gift certificate for a pottery class
- ⊰ A handmade vase or fruit bowl
- ⊰ A gift certificate to a local pottery studio or to Pottery Barn
- ⊰ A personalized cookie jar filled with homemade cookies
- ⊰ A plant in a beautiful painted pot

YEAR: 10
Tradition: Tin

Gift Suggestions:

- A set of tin cookie cutters and decorating supplies
- A tin toy car to announce a romantic road trip
- A gift wrapped in aluminum foil

 YEAR: 11
Tradition: Steel

Gift Suggestions:

- A cocktail shaker, a cocktail recipe book, and a few choice liqueurs
- A new stainless steel appliance or a set of cookware
- A pair of steel harmonicas and a book on how to play

 YEAR: 12
Tradition: Silk

Gift Suggestions:

- Silk pajamas or sheets
- A silk tie or scarf
- A custom silk-screened T-shirt or piece of art

⋄ **A silk eye pillow and a day of pampering**

⋄ **Silk long underwear and a skiing trip**

YEAR: 13

Tradition: Lace

Gift Suggestions:

⋄ **Lace lingerie**

⋄ **A lace tablecloth or table runner, plus a romantic dinner**

⋄ **A lace invitation to an evening at a Victorian bed-and-breakfast**

YEAR: 14

Tradition: Ivory

Ivory is the traditional symbol of the fourteenth anniversary. Due to illegal trading in elephant ivory, however, buying ivory is no longer advised—unless it's antique. Mother-of-pearl makes a great substitute.

Gift Suggestions:

⋄ **A piano or piano lessons for two**

⋄ **An evening out at a local piano bar**

⋄ **An ivory-colored set of sheets and breakfast in bed**

⋄ **A set of mother-of-pearl candlesticks and a gift certificate for dinner for two**

⌁ A donation in the couple's names to a wildlife preservation fund

YEAR: 15
Tradition: Crystal

Gift Suggestions:

⌁ Two engraved crystal champagne flutes and a bottle of champagne

⌁ A trip to a fortune-teller to have a look in a crystal ball

⌁ A crystal vase filled with favorite flowers

⌁ Crystal wineglasses and a subscription to a wine-of-the-month club

YEAR: 20
Tradition: China

Gift Suggestions:

⌁ Any china pieces the couple may be missing

⌁ A selection of teas and a china teapot

⌁ A piece of jewelry in a Chinese take-out container

⌁ A gift certificate to a Chinese restaurant

⌁ A trip to China

YEAR: 25
Tradition: Silver

Gift Suggestions:

- A silver photo album or frame with photos from the couple's twenty-five years

- A silver bracelet for her with the birthstones of children and grandchildren

- An engraved silver money clip or business card holder for him

- A set of two silver dollars, one from the year of the wedding and one from today

- A silver car

YEAR: 30
Tradition: Pearl

Gift Suggestions:

- A pearl necklace

- Scuba-diving lessons

- A seafood dinner featuring mollusks and oysters

- A collection of "pearls of wisdom" you've gathered from your spouse or parents over the years, captured in an album or journal

YEAR: 35
Tradition: Coral

Gift Suggestions:

- ◁ A trip to Hawaii or Australia where coral reefs are abundant (present the gift with a piece of dried coral)
- ◁ Coral jewelry
- ◁ A coral sculpture
- ◁ A freshwater aquarium filled with a variety of fish and coral pieces

 ## YEAR: 40
Tradition: Ruby

Gift Suggestions:

- ◁ Ruby jewelry
- ◁ Ruby slippers for her and a copy of *The Wizard of Oz* for him, to remind them there's no place like home
- ◁ A bottle of vintage red wine
- ◁ A dozen ruby red roses
- ◁ A ruby added to your wedding bands
- ◁ A pair of red pajamas
- ◁ A ruby red glass vase or bowl

Tradition: Sapphire

Gift Suggestions:

- ⊰ **Sapphire jewelry**
- ⊰ **A tropical vacation to gaze upon the deep blue sea**
- ⊰ **A coffee-table book featuring Picasso's Blue Period, with tickets for a trip to Spain slipped inside**
- ⊰ **A deep-blue glass vase or bowl**

Tradition: Gold

Gift Suggestions:

- ⊰ **A gold photo frame with two pictures: one of the couple on their wedding day and one from today**
- ⊰ **Paper is the tradition for first wedding anniversaries; collect paper memorabilia from the couple's fifty years together (photos, newspaper clippings, letters) and put them together in a gold album.**
- ⊰ **A gold engraved pocket watch or locket**
- ⊰ **A golden oldies CD with the couple's favorite songs from the past fifty years**
- ⊰ **A bedroom makeover featuring gold accents (sheets, pillows, etc.)**
- ⊰ **A trip to the Gold Coast**
- ⊰ **A gold car**

New Arrivals

Everybody loves a new baby. And the joy of this precious occasion spreads like ripples across a pond from parents to grandparents, friends, neighbors, and coworkers.

There are very few gift-giving occasions that provide more pleasure than shopping for those adorable bundles of joy. Walk into any baby store (or baby section for that matter) and you'll experience an onslaught of cute and irresistible. The pint-size shoes and teeny-tiny clothes can be tempting, but it's important to keep the nature of babies in mind. At the rate they grow, their parents will be lucky if the little one wears the snazzy duds twice.

So how can you give a gift that will be cherished for years and not outgrown in a few months? Easy. Make sure it has meaning. Whether it's a bronzed pair of baby shoes or an engraved silver spoon, meaningful gifts often become family heirlooms and are passed along to future generations. I vividly remember a quilt my great aunt made for me when I was born (each square a different appliquéd animal). It now lives in a carefully packed box and will undoubtedly have a prominent home in my firstborn's bedroom.

But, like wedding registries, baby registries exist for a reason. New parents are typically overwhelmed by the things they need, so it's smart to package tradition and meaning with a good dose of practicality. Chests are symbolic of treasure, and wood represents new beginnings. Why not give a personalized toy box or blanket chest? It's an heirloom piece of furniture and a great place to stash all of baby's belongings.

You might also consider waiting until after the baby is born to give a gift. You'll know the sex, the name, and maybe even a bit about the little one's personality, which makes selecting the perfect meaningful gift (and personalizing it) that much easier.

And don't forget about Mom and Dad. With all the baby hubbub, they'll appreciate something special and "just for them."

 BASKET
Symbolizes abundance, fertility

Full baskets symbolize the womb and abundance. When wool or fruit is inside, they can also be a symbol of fertility.

Gift Suggestions:

- A Moses basket filled with sleep-themed items, like a blanket, a stuffed animal, and a lullaby CD or book
- A basket of baby essentials or small items from the registry
- A basket of fragrance-free lotions and potions for Mom and baby

BATH
Symbolizes cleansing, purity, relaxation

Throughout history, water has been granted transformative qualities that border on magic. Baths relax and are thought to clean both the body and the soul.

Gift Suggestions:

- A baby bathtub filled with bath products for baby, like washcloths, soap, lotion, and a personalized hooded towel
- A hand-knitted washcloth or two, packaged with some all-natural cleanser and a rubber duck or other bath toys
- A basket of relaxing bath products for Mom

BELL
Symbolizes protection

In many cultures, parents tied bells to their newborn's hands, feet, or cradle to protect the baby from evil spirits. In the early twentieth century, teething rings often featured bells for the same reason.

Gift Suggestions:

- An engraved bell holiday ornament
- A pair of newborn baby booties or a hat with tiny bells sewn on
- A sterling silver rattle

⭸ **A special edition of *Peter Pan*, featuring the one and only Tinker Bell**

 BOOK
Symbolizes knowledge, wisdom, the universe

Books are a bottomless well of knowledge and wisdom and often a symbol of high culture. In a sense, they represent the universe and all it holds.

Gift Suggestions:

⭸ **A baby book or photo album**

⭸ **A classic children's book with an inscription inside**

⭸ **A book of lullabies or sing-along songs**

⭸ **Your favorite book from childhood**

⭸ **A subscription to a parenting magazine (or even a fun celebrity gossip magazine to read in between feedings)**

 BRONZE
Symbolizes preservation

Parents in America have been bronzing baby shoes to remember their little one's first steps since the 1930s.

Gift Suggestion:

⭸ **A certificate for bronzing down the road. Though shoes are the most commonly bronzed item, just about anything can be bronzed, including baby bottles and pacifiers.**

CHAMOMILE
Symbolizes calmness, sleep

In aromatherapy, chamomile has calming properties. It promotes sleep and eases tension—just what new parents need.

Gift Suggestions:

- ৵ **Chamomile tea and a teapot for Mom**
- ৵ **A selection of chamomile bath products for baby and parents**
- ৵ **A baby blanket and a chamomile sachet**

 ## CHEST
Symbolizes treasure, revelation

Chests, or coffers, hold treasure to be revealed at a later date and are often associated with the heart. Famous coffers include the Ark of the Covenant, which held the Ten Commandments, and Pandora's box, keeper of hope.

Gift Suggestions:

- ৵ **A time capsule: Collect current pictures, magazines, and other signs of the time of birth; seal them up in a box or other small container with a note for the baby to open it on a future birthday.**
- ৵ **A personalized toy or blanket chest**
- ৵ **A small chest for baby's shelf to store treasures (lock of hair, first tooth, etc.)**

A MENAGERIE OF MEANING

Most (if not all) animals are symbolic. Here are a few of the most appropriate for newborn gift giving.

BEAR
Symbolizes power, strength, sons, motherliness

Known for their motherly instincts, bears are seen in many cultures as a symbol of power and strength. In China, dreaming of a bear is a sign that you'll give birth to a son.

HIPPOPOTAMUS
Symbolizes fertility, motherhood

In Egyptian mythology, the goddess Taueret symbolized fertility and had the head of a hippo. Figurines of the goddess were placed near women giving birth for good luck.

STORK
Symbolizes fertility, birth, parental instincts

Storks carrying babies are a common image in pop culture (and a convenient explanation for where babies come from). This may have come from the belief that, as waterbirds, storks frequented the "waters of creation." Storks are not only good parents to their young, but good children to their parents, taking care of them in their old age.

TIGER
Symbolizes protection, courage, strength

Tigers symbolize courage and strength. In China, they are thought to have protective qualities, and some children are given tiger caps or shoes for this reason.

Gift Suggestions:

- ⊰ **A stuffed animal**
- ⊰ **Clothing featuring the symbolic animal**
- ⊰ **A blanket or quilt with the animal (or animals) appliquéd or embroidered**
- ⊰ **An animal adopted in the baby's name**

DAISY
Symbolizes innocence, luck

The dainty flower represents innocence and is traditionally given to moms to wish them good luck in childbirth. In France, it's common for Mom to receive daisies from her husband and her father after the baby's born.

Gift Suggestions:

- ⊰ **A bouquet of daisies for the hospital**
- ⊰ **A bouquet of daisies in an engraved silver vase**
- ⊰ **A receiving blanket or quilt embroidered with daisies**

DATE
Symbolizes birth, fertility, offspring

Mary was thought to have given birth under a date palm, using the fruit from the tree to ease labor pains. The date is also considered a symbol of fertility and is representative of offspring.

Gift Suggestions:

- A basket of fresh Medjool dates for the parents
- Fresh-baked date bread
- A date palm for the family's yard

  ### EGG
Symbolizes fertility, luck, immortality, speech

A popular symbol of fertility, eggs are given as baby gifts in several countries: in China for good luck, in England for immortality, and in Germany to encourage early speech.

Gift Suggestions:

- A frozen homemade quiche for the new parents
- A copy of *The Golden Goose* or a collection of Mother Goose stories
- A piggy bank for the baby to build her nest egg
- A golden egg baby rattle

GEODE
Symbolizes healthy pregnancy, fertility

Geodes are pieces of stones lined on the inside with crystals. They're said to promote conception and increase fertility when placed in the bedroom, and carrying them is thought to prevent miscarriages and ensure a successful birth.

Gift Suggestions:

- **A geode the color of the baby's anticipated birthstone for Mom to keep bedside**
- **A piece of geode jewelry for Mom to wear before and during the birth**

MOTHER-OF-PEARL
Symbolizes protection, balance, fertility, nurturing

Though this stone is thought to protect anyone who wears it, it's especially effective on babies and children, safeguarding their emotional well-being. It also nurtures the soul and promotes balance, fertility, and wholeness.

Gift Suggestions:

- **A mother-of-pearl photo frame**
- **A rattle with a mother-of-pearl handle**
- **A simple handmade baby bracelet with the baby's name and mother-of-pearl beads**

POTTERY
Symbolizes procreation, fertility

Khnum was an Egyptian god who created the spirit and body of every child out of clay on his potter's wheel.

Gift Suggestions:

- ⌁ **A personalized plate or mug for the new child**
- ⌁ **A handmade vase with daisies for the delivery room**
- ⌁ **A decorative clay pot, jar, or plaque for the baby's room**
- ⌁ **A kit for preserving the child's handprints in clay**

PUMICE
Symbolizes easy childbirth, protection

This volcanic rock has a protective quality and an ability to absorb negative energy. At one time, it was pressed into the palms of birthing mothers to ease childbirth.

Gift Suggestions:

- ⌁ **A pedicure gift certificate for Mom**
- ⌁ **A basket full of items to pamper the parents, like bubble bath, pumice foot scrub, and lotion**

SILVER
Symbolizes luck, fortune, purity

Silver spoons were once given as baby gifts to promote wealth, and the tradition may have contributed to the expression "born with a silver spoon in your mouth." In Scotland and Ireland, it's customary to cross a baby's palm with silver for good luck. Silver also symbolizes purity and balance.

Gift Suggestions:

- **An engraved silver baby spoon or cup**
- **Silver baby jewelry**
- **A silver baby brush and comb set**
- **An engraved Tiffany silver rattle**
- **Commemorative silver coins from the year of baby's birth**
- **A silver locket with photo of the baby for Mom**

 WOOD

Symbolizes life, strength, honor

Wood represents new beginnings and life. In ancient times, Jewish families would plant a tree in honor of the newborn child. The wood from the tree (cedar for boys and cypress or pine for girls) was used for the wedding canopy when the child was ready to marry.

Gift Suggestions:

- **A wooden music box**
- **A toy box**
- **A small rocking chair or rocking horse**
- **A personalized stepping stool**

- A small tree for the yard to grow with the child
- A wooden toy set you can add to every year, like Noah's ark or a train set

Housewarming

If you've ever moved into a new house, you know it's both exhilarating and stressful. You're thrilled about your new place and starting "fresh," but along with the good feelings come a few not-so-good feelings, like anxiety and uncertainty. Perhaps you're new to town and you've left your friends and family behind. Your favorite things are in boxes, and your mile-long to-do list includes everything from "find new dentist" to "find nearest grocery store." Maybe your kids are nervous about attending a new school . . . or the first night's sleep in a new house. Just when you start questioning your move, there's a knock on your door. It's your new neighbor with a small gift in hand. Her smiling face and kind gesture are an oasis in a sea of cardboard boxes. Your mood is instantly lifted. You're suddenly feeling a bit more settled.

I'm sure you've heard the phrase "it's the thought that counts," and never were truer words spoken. Housewarming gifts, no matter how big or small, are always appreciated by people settling into a new place. Offerings of peace, protection, and prosperity not only help people feel warm and cozy in their new homes, they also help build friendships and communities. And it's a lovely opportunity for a meaningful gift since the occasion is rife with tradition.

Welcoming families into their homes with a symbolic gift dates back hundreds of years, and nearly every culture has its own tradition. You may even remember the scene from *It's a Wonderful Life*, where George and Mary usher an Italian immigrant family, the Martinis, into their new home. Mary stands at the doorstep with an armful of gifts and proclaims, "Bread—that this house may never know hunger. Salt—that life may always have flavor. Wine—that joy and prosperity may reign forever." Other traditions throw a broom or a candle into the mix to sweep away evil spirits and ensure the new home is always filled with light.

A list of traditional housewarming gifts follows, and though tradition goes a long way to create a meaningful gift, a personal, twenty-first-century spin doesn't hurt. Salt has been given for generations as a symbol of variety and prosperity, but that doesn't mean you can (or should) wrap a ribbon around a saltshaker and call it good. Try incorporating the traditional gift into a useful and meaningful package for the new home. Grab a favorite cookbook or a copy of a family recipe and give it alongside a fancy package of flavored salt. Other gifts, however, can stand on their own. A jar of gourmet honey, for instance, wishes the new homeowners a sweet life.

What you give depends largely on how well you know the person and the individual situation. A family of four moving into a larger home will have very different needs than a recent college graduate moving into a bachelor pad or empty nesters downsizing into a low-maintenance condo. For good friends, you can pick something according to their tastes and personality. But, if you don't know the person well and aren't sure

if they're into Monet or M. C. Escher, it's a good bet to stick with consumable gifts, like wine or food.

And remember, housewarming gifts don't need to be wrapped in the traditional sense. Use a basket (which has its own special meaning) or a simple ribbon and don't forget the handwritten note. If possible, take the gift to the new home so you can share your welcoming wishes in person.

ALOE VERA
Symbolizes good luck, protection

In Hawaii, aloe vera symbolizes good luck and is said to protect homes from intruders and negative energy. The plant also has healing qualities and is often kept in the home and applied to burns, cuts, and scrapes.

Gift Suggestions:

- **A potted aloe vera plant along with a first aid kit for the home**
- **A basket of aloe vera lotion, hand soaps, or candles**

BASKET
Symbolizes wholeness, abundance, wisdom, liberation

In ancient Egypt, baskets symbolized wholeness and, when full, abundance. In Native American cultures, they were placed by the front door so guests could leave their worries outside. In New Zealand, the Maori basket, or *kete*, symbolizes a container for knowledge and wisdom and represents the group's liberation from Western culture.

Gift Suggestions:

- ☙ **A woven laundry basket filled with various organic or nicely scented cleaning supplies**
- ☙ **A small basket filled with helpful information about the area. Include take-out menus, a gift certificate to a local restaurant, personalized address labels, movie theater tickets, and local magazines. You can even make your own map of the neighborhood that includes all the best places to eat, shop, and play.**
- ☙ **A basket filled with other symbolic housewarming gifts, like bread, salt, wine, and a candle**
- ☙ **A basket with all the fixings for a delicious breakfast or dinner**

BEE

Symbolizes work, obedience, abundance, sweetness

Bees are busy symbols. Traditionally, they symbolize work, abundance, and obedience. The fruit of their labor—honey—represents fertility, preservation, and sweetness and is often referred to as "heavenly dew." Honey is a traditional housewarming gift (like salt, bread, or wine) symbolizing a "sweet" life.

Gift Suggestions:

- ☙ **A jar of gourmet honey and a loaf of fresh-baked bread**

⇛ A handful of flavored honey sticks tied with a green bow to represent hope and joy

⇛ A set of beeswax or honey-scented candles

⇛ A selection of honey-themed breakfast items in a basket. Include a loaf of bread, flavored honey, and Honey-Comb cereal.

BIRD
Symbolizes strength, fertility, soul

In some cultures, birds are thought to carry the souls of ancestors. Bird-themed gifts were presented to new homeowners to give the home soul and depth. They symbolize fertility and strength in Africa.

Gift Suggestions:

⇛ A bare-wood birdhouse and the supplies to decorate it

⇛ A coffee-table book featuring beautiful birds

⇛ A hummingbird feeder or birdhouse

BREAD
Symbolizes nourishment, abundance, hospitality

One of the most widespread symbols of hospitality, bread represents both spiritual and physical nourishment and is often given with salt and wine. There's a Moroccan proverb that says, "By bread and salt we are united."

Gift Suggestions:

- ☙ **A gift certificate to a local bakery**
- ☙ **A bread machine and a package of fancy dough mix**
- ☙ **A loaf of local bakery bread with gourmet jam**
- ☙ **Homemade banana or other bread, with a recipe card**
- ☙ **A copy of *It's a Wonderful Life*, along with bread, salt, and wine**

BRICK

Symbolizes security, settlement, community

Bricks symbolize settlement. They're used to build homes and towns, which in turn build communities and friendships.

Gift Suggestions:

- ☙ **Buy a brick from your local home and garden store, write the date on the back of it, decorate it if you'd like, and present it as a doorstop for the new home.**
- ☙ **An engraved brick stepping stone for the yard. Include the family's name and the date.**

BROOM

Symbolizes renewal, cleanliness, protection

Brooms have a long history of cultural significance, sweeping away the old to make room for the new. In ancient shrines, sweeping was an act of worship, and there's an old

superstition that says you should never take an old broom into a new house.

Gift Suggestions:

- **A handcrafted broom and a subscription to a home magazine**
- **A gift certificate for a cleaning service**
- **A basket with a broom, dustpan, and various cleaning supplies**
- **A personalized hearth broom**

CACTUS
Symbolizes protection

Native Americans planted cacti at each corner of the home to guard against negative influences.

Gift Suggestion:

- **A Christmas cactus or other potted cactus for the home or porch**

CANDLE
Symbolizes light, warmth, faith

One of the traditional housewarming gifts, candles are given to provide light and warmth to the new home.

Gift Suggestion:

- ☙ Use the colors of popular magic to emblaze your gift with even more meaning. White offers peace, household purification, and spirituality; green brings luck, prosperity, and healing energy; pink promotes love and friendship; and blue provides prophetic dreams and protection while sleeping.

CASTLE

Symbolizes protection, spirit, pride

The proverbial expression "A man's home is his castle" holds true. A castle is a place of protection and retreat, just like one's home. An enchanted place in fairy tales, castles also represent safekeeping of one's inner spiritual being.

Gift Suggestions:

- ☙ A rubber return-address stamp with an image of a castle
- ☙ A coffee-table book featuring images of stunning castles. Take a picture of the family's new house and paste it on the inside front cover along with your inscription welcoming them into their new "castle."

CLOCK

Symbolizes transition, new beginnings, discovery

Clocks represent the passing of time. They remind us that nothing is constant but change and help ring in a new phase of

our lives. As one of the most important inventions of ancient man, they also symbolize innovation and discovery.

Gift Suggestions:

- **A clock for the new home**
- **A kitchen timer**

COINS
Symbolize wealth, luck, peace

In Britain, lucky sixpences are given for many occasions, including welcoming a family into a new home. Silver is also thought to harbor a peaceful energy.

Gift Suggestion:

- **For someone in an apartment, a nice jar or container that reflects the recipient's personality, filled with quarters for laundry or parking**

HERBS
Symbolize protection, purity

A variety of herbs are used in traditional household smudging, including sage, rosemary, bay, myrtle, sandalwood, and frankincense. Herbs are dried, tied into bundles, and set on fire. The smoke is spread throughout the house to drive away evil spirits and clean the energy of the home.

Gift Suggestions:

- ⊰ **An herb wreath for the front door**
- ⊰ **Small terra-cotta pots with a variety of herbs to be used as a windowsill herb garden**
- ⊰ **A selection of dried herbs, salt and pepper, and olive oil and vinegar, along with a loaf of bread**
- ⊰ **A smudge stick and a book on smudging or spiritual housecleaning**

HORSESHOE
Symbolizes good luck, protection

One of the most well-known good luck charms, horseshoes were often hung over doorways as protective amulets. Some believed that you should hang the horseshoe upside down so that the luck wouldn't drain out.

Gift Suggestions:

- ⊰ **A horseshoe door knocker**
- ⊰ **An engraved or painted horseshoe with the family's name and/or new address**

HOUSE
Symbolizes humanity, self, protection

A home is a place for both rest and celebration, for solitude and socializing. It's an early symbol of humanity from which all other structures were born, including cities. According to

psychologist Carl Jung, what happens inside the house happens within ourselves.

Gift Suggestion:

⊰ Visit your local assessor's office and order an archived picture of the person's new home. Present it in a frame.

JAR
Symbolizes abundance, wealth, pleasure

Referred to historically as casks, jars represent a well of wealth and pleasure.

Gift Suggestions:

⊰ Give a decorative jar filled with hot cocoa mix, pickled foods, or jam.

⊰ Have your family write fun things to do in the neighborhood on small slips of paper. Put them in a jar, wrap a bow around it, and present it to the new homeowners. Whenever they're looking for entertainment, they'll reach into your jar and pull out an idea.

KEY
Symbolizes happiness, liberation, power, status

Across the world, the key represents ownership of property, which suggests power and status. A Japanese symbol of happiness, keys allow you to open and close freely and therefore provide liberation. Naturally, it's a perfect gift for a new homeowner.

Gift Suggestions:

- ⭐ **An engraved key chain**
- ⭐ **A fancy glass bowl that can be placed by the door for keys**

PINEAPPLE
Symbolizes hospitality

Pineapples are a widespread symbol of hospitality. For years, they were a rare culinary treat in most parts of the world and were used in centerpieces by well-to-do families when visitors were expected. Legend says that U.S. sailors would place pineapples on their gateposts to let neighbors know that the man of the house had returned from sea. Today, the pineapple motif still appears on linens, doors and gates, draperies, and other household items as a welcoming symbol.

Gift Suggestions:

- ⭐ **A fresh pineapple**
- ⭐ **A festive doormat with pineapples on it**
- ⭐ **All the fixings for piña coladas, including ingredients, pineapple napkins, and pineapple swizzle sticks or straws**
- ⭐ **A pineapple-scented candle or guest soaps**

SALT

Symbolizes decency, protection, purification, flavor

For years, salt was considered to be a precious and rare commodity, used as a currency in Rome. People who are referred to as "the salt of the earth" are said to be decent and dependable. As a housewarming tradition, salt is believed to protect, purify, and cleanse the home, as well as ensure the residents' lives are full of flavor.

Gift Suggestions:

- ⊰ **A cookbook or selection of your favorite family recipes and a package of kosher salt**
- ⊰ **A selection of gourmet flavored sea salts**
- ⊰ **A copy of *It's a Wonderful Life*, along with bread, salt, and wine**
- ⊰ **A jar of bath salts**

WINE

Symbolizes life, youth, prosperity

Viewed as a spiritual drink, wine is a symbol of youth and eternal life. When given as a housewarming gift, it symbolizes a joyful and prosperous life in the new home.

Gift Suggestions:

- ⊰ **A bottle of wine**

- A special bottle of wine to be opened on the first, fifth, or tenth anniversary in their new home. Include the family's name and the date on the bottle or on a special box or bag to store it in.
- Wine accoutrements, like an opener, decanter, or wine-glass tags
- A copy of *It's a Wonderful Life*, along with bread, salt, and wine

WOOD

Symbolizes new beginnings, the heart, protection

Wood is said to guard against hunger and evil. It represents new beginnings and helps to feed the fire in the hearth, which is the heart of the home.

Gift Suggestions:

- A basket of firewood
- A tree for the family's yard
- A wooden game, like chess or backgammon
- A wooden welcome sign for the new house

Christmas

Originally a celebration of the birth of Jesus Christ, the season of giving has, for many, become the season of too much stuff. The commercialization of the holiday makes it a welcome candidate for a meaningful gift to help spread the true sentiments of the season: peace, love, and goodwill toward all.

ANGEL

Symbolizes good tidings, protection

Angels are heavenly symbols who can take human form and are thought to be messengers of good news. They make great gifts for the "angels" in your life.

Gift Suggestions:

- An engraved angel ornament or tree topper
- A handkerchief, scarf, apron, or tea towel embroidered with angels
- A holiday brooch or other jewelry with an angel motif
- A coffee-table book of angel art
- A mixed CD with songs featuring the word "angel," like "Angel" (Sarah McLachlan), "She Talks to Angels"

(The Black Crowes), "Sweet Angel" (Jimi Hendrix), and "Earth Angel" (The Penguins)

BOOK
Symbolizes knowledge, wisdom

Books are a bottomless well of knowledge and wisdom and often a symbol of high culture. In a sense, they represent the universe and all it holds.

Gift Suggestions:

- ❧ Special editions of holiday books for adults and kids, such as *A Christmas Carol*, by Charles Dickens; *Olivia Helps with Christmas*, by Ian Falconer; *The Night Before Christmas*, by Clement C. Moore; or *The Polar Express*, by Chris Van Allsburg
- ❧ A holiday cookbook with Christmas cookie cutters
- ❧ A journal for the upcoming year
- ❧ A guest book or album for recording visitors to the home each Christmas

CANDLESTICK
Symbolizes God, light

Candles and candlesticks play an important part in many religious celebrations. In Jewish tradition, the menorah represents the eyes of God, and in Christianity, a lit candle symbolizes Christ as the light of the world.

Gift Suggestions:

- ☙ **A set of silver candlesticks with red and green scented candles**
- ☙ **A table centerpiece that includes candlesticks given a few weeks prior to Christmas, so it can be enjoyed throughout the festivities**

CHEST
Symbolizes treasure, revealed secrets

Chests, or coffers, hold treasure to be revealed at a later date. Containers like this are also often associated with the heart. Famous coffers include the Ark of the Covenant, which held the Ten Commandments, and Pandora's box, keeper of hope.

Gift Suggestions:

- ☙ **A time capsule of the year (for an individual or the whole family) to be opened at a later date**
- ☙ **A personalized box to house special Christmas ornaments or decorations**
- ☙ **A jewelry box with a special piece of jewelry inside**

CHESTNUT
Symbolizes goodness, chastity, tradition

Greeks honored the chestnut and referred to it as the "acorn of Zeus." In Christian tradition, they represent goodness and chastity. Roasted chestnuts are a holiday tradition for many families and are memorialized in the classic tune "The Christmas Song."

Gift Suggestions:

- ⊰ **A bag of chestnuts, a batch of figgy pudding, and a holiday CD that includes "The Christmas Song"**
- ⊰ **A bag of chestnuts, a chestnut roaster, and a chestnut-colored blanket to cuddle by the fire**
- ⊰ **A chestnut tree**

DRUM

Symbolizes truth, harmony, worship, Mother Earth

Drums are often regarded as the heartbeat of Mother Earth. They symbolize divine truth and are used by Native Americans in ceremonies as a way to celebrate and connect to Mother Earth.

Gift Suggestions:

- ⊰ **A drum set and drum lessons**
- ⊰ **Tickets to a rock concert**
- ⊰ **A decorative drum**
- ⊰ **Child-size bongo drums for a family with children**

FRANKINCENSE AND MYRRH
Symbolize tradition, spirit

The three wise men brought gold, frankincense, and myrrh to baby Jesus in the Bible. Frankincense and myrrh were rare and expensive gum, or resin, from trees. They were dried and burned and used in worship, for medicinal purposes, and as a perfume.

Gift Suggestions:

- **Frankincense and myrrh incense wrapped with a gold ribbon**
- **Frankincense or myrrh perfume or essential oils**

FRUITCAKE
Symbolizes fertility

Though the concept of the fruitcake dates back as far as ancient Egypt, it first appeared regularly in Europe in the 1700s. The fruits and nuts symbolized fertility and hopes for a plentiful harvest the upcoming year.

Gift Suggestions:

- **A fruitcake (of course)**
- **A subscription to a fruit-of-the-month club**
- **A cake dish and a gift certificate for whatever type of homemade cake they'd like**

HOLLY

Symbolizes sacrifice, goodwill

Romans decked the halls with holly during their winter solstice celebration, Saturnalia, and gave each other boughs as a symbol of goodwill. For Christians, the plant serves as a reminder of Christ's sacrifice, representing the crown of thorns.

Gift Suggestions:

- **A holly wreath, centerpiece, or swag**
- **Holly berry candles**

MISTLETOE

Symbolizes love, immortality, protection, peace

Mistletoe was considered a sacred plant in ancient times. In France, it was left under beds to discourage nightmares, and the Norse thought it represented peace. Today, if two people find themselves standing under this magical plant, they're destined to kiss. Because it's an evergreen, mistletoe was thought to be a symbol of immortality.

Gift Suggestions:

- **A holiday love note, tied with a ribbon and a sprig of mistletoe**
- **A mistletoe wreath**

OLIVE
Symbolizes immortality, peace, hope

In the Bible, the dove left the ark and returned with an olive branch in his beak. This symbolized the end of the flood and peace with God. Greenpeace, an organization devoted to protecting the environment and promoting peace, uses a dove carrying an olive branch as its emblem. Olive branches were also an attribute of Pax, the Roman goddess of peace.

Gift Suggestions:

- **An olive tree for the recipient's yard**
- **A selection of gourmet olives and a loaf of bread**
- **An item carved from olive wood such as an ornament, a candleholder, a bowl, or a nativity set**
- **A bottle of gourmet olive oil**

 POETRY
Symbolizes tradition

In the Netherlands, Christmas gifts are often accompanied by a poem from Sinterklaas (Santa Claus). The rhymes are humorous and meant to cause some good-natured embarrassment for the recipient.

Gift Suggestions:

- **A poem with a donation in the recipient's name to a favorite charity**

- A small meaningful item, such as an ornament, and a related poem
- A book of poetry

SHOES
Symbolize respect, anticipation

In France, Germany, and the Netherlands, kids place polished shoes by their bed or the chimney in hopes they'll be filled with trinkets in the morning. Taking off one's shoes when entering a house is a sign of respect.

Gift Suggestion:

- A new pair of shoes, slippers, or boots, filled with small surprises

WINE
Symbolizes life, youth

A representation of blood, wine is universally a symbol of youth and eternal life. In Islam, it represents both love and wisdom.

Gift Suggestions:

- A special bottle of wine in an engraved wooden box
- Wine accoutrements, like an opener, decanter, or wine-glass tags
- A bottle of wine with a personalized holiday label

Valentine's Day

Though there are numerous tales of the origination of Valentine's Day, many believe it was an ode to several historical Valentines, one of which was Priest Valentine, a champion of love who secretly married forbidden couples. February 14 is also said to be the day that birds select their mate, and historically some extravagant gifts have been exchanged by lovebirds, from palaces to rare jewels. But you don't have to be extravagant to express your love and sincere affection. Think small, romantic, honest, and meaningful.

BOOK
Symbolizes knowledge, wisdom

Books are a bottomless well of knowledge and wisdom and often a symbol of high culture. In a sense, they represent the universe and all it holds.

Gift Suggestions:

- **A book of love poetry to read together**
- **A photo album or scrapbook celebrating your favorite moments together**
- **A first edition or signed copy of her favorite book**

◁ A copy of a classic romantic novel, like *Love in the Time of Cholera*, by Gabriel García Márquez, or *Pride and Prejudice*, by Jane Austen, and an invitation to a romantic dinner

CHOCOLATE
Symbolizes luxury, love, richness

Once considered an expensive luxury, chocolate is often associated with romance and is thought to be an aphrodisiac. Aztec priests drank chocolate as part of sacred ceremonies.

Gift Suggestions:

◁ Homemade chocolate cake, cupcakes, or truffles

◁ A bag of personalized M&Ms

◁ A gift box of chocolate from an artisanal maker and a copy of *Chocolat* (the book, by Joanne Harris, or a DVD of the movie)

◁ A cocktail shaker, a set of martini glasses, and a chocolate liqueur

◁ A chocolate-scented massage bar and a book on massage

◁ Breakfast in bed featuring chocolate chip pancakes and hot chocolate

CUPID
Symbolizes earthly love

Also known as Eros, Cupid represented earthly love. He shot

his victims with his bow and arrow, causing them to fall for each other.

Gift Suggestions:

- ↲ **A handmade card using a variety of love symbols, like Cupid, doves, and hearts**
- ↲ **A Cupid pin, pendant, or figurine**

DOVE
Symbolizes peace, purity, love

In the Bible, a dove was sent from the ark and it came back carrying an olive branch. Since then, doves have been seen as a sign of peace and a symbol of innocence, love, and purity. Two doves together are often used as a symbol of marital bliss.

Gift Suggestions:

- ↲ **A selection of Dove chocolates and a night on the town**
- ↲ **A trip to a local aviary**
- ↲ **A handmade card using a variety of love symbols, like Cupid, doves, and hearts**

FLOWERS
Symbolize various meanings

See Appendix A: The Meaning of Flowers & Trees (pg. 125) for a list of flowers and their meanings. Roses are the traditional Valentine's Day flower.

LOVELY FRUITS

Fruit is a sweet (and meaningful!) way to express your love.

APPLE
Symbolizes love, fertility

Although in the Bible this fruit represents temptation, it also symbolizes love and fertility. One of the first fruits gathered by man, it's an emblem of Venus, and, according to myth, was created by Dionysus, the god of intoxication.

APRICOT
Symbolizes femininity, good fortune, love

Dreaming of apricots is supposedly an omen of good fortune and love, and for the Europeans, is thought to be an aphrodisiac.

CHERRY
Symbolizes youth, protection, femininity

In ancient China, the wood of the cherry tree was thought to ward off evil spirits. The cherry blossom is an important symbol in Japan, representing youth, beauty, and femininity.

FIG
Symbolizes fertility, abundance

In Rome, the fig is thought to symbolize fertility. Its many seeds represent abundance and prosperity, and its

leaves suggest the minimal clothing worn by Adam and Eve.

Gift Suggestions:

- ⊰ **A basket of fruit or fruit jams, with each item representing a specific strength: apricot for good fortune, apple for love, and cherry for beauty**
- ⊰ **A small basket of fruit-scented essential oils and candles**
- ⊰ **A fruit tree (or a gift certificate for one from a nursery)**
- ⊰ **A subscription to a fruit-of-the-month club**
- ⊰ **A basket with fruit-scented lotions and bubble bath**
- ⊰ **A romantic meal featuring a variety of symbolic fruits**

HEART
Symbolizes love, spirit

Hearts are the classic symbol of love, adorning everything from T-shirts to cards to biceps. In many cultures, the heart is thought to be the center of thought, feeling, and spirit.

Gift Suggestions:

- ⊰ **A handmade card using a variety of love symbols, like Cupid, doves, and hearts**

- A booklet of heart-shaped IOU coupons
- A batch of heart-shaped sugar cookies decorated with special messages
- A handblown glass heart paperweight or ornament
- A bowl of heart candies, or a heart-shaped box of chocolates, with a small gift hidden inside

JASMINE
Symbolizes love, happiness

This fragrant flower is the Hindu symbol for love and was often carried in bridal bouquets. In Christianity, it represents happiness.

Gift Suggestions:

- A set of indulgent sheets and jasmine-scented linen spray
- A tea set for two and jasmine tea
- A basket with jasmine body spray, lotion, and bubble bath

OYSTER
Symbolizes sexuality, secrecy

Long considered an aphrodisiac, oysters are a symbol of female sexuality and fertility. Their tightly sealed shell also suggests secrecy.

Gift Suggestions:

- A string of pearls or pearl earrings
- A romantic dinner at a seafood restaurant
- A meal of champagne and oysters at home

STARFISH
Symbolizes pure love, regeneration, rebirth

Starfish thrive in the sea and represent powerful, eternal love. The starfish also symbolizes regeneration and rebirth. *Stella Maris*, Latin for "star of the sea," is another title for the Virgin Mary.

Gift Suggestions:

- Snorkeling gear and a surprise vacation
- A silver starfish pendant
- An aquarium membership
- A weekend getaway to a nearby city, with a visit to its aquarium or beaches
- A chartered boat or ferry ride to go tide pooling

Mother's Day

From Japan to Australia to India, nearly all countries have some version of Mother's Day. The celebrations vary, but most include flowers, meals, cards, phone calls, and in-person visits to Mom.

Though the earliest celebrations likely took place in ancient Greece to honor Rhea, mother of Greek gods, the first officially documented Mother's Day event was on May 10, 1908, in West Virginia. It was arranged by Anna M. Jarvis in remembrance of her mother. Her mother's favorite flowers, white carnations, were given to every mother in attendance.

As far as gifts are concerned, most moms would agree that all Mother's Day presents are meaningful, whether it's an elaborate bouquet of flowers or a macaroni necklace.

 BED
Symbolizes renewal, rest, birth, family

Beds are a symbol of sleep but have, at one time or another, been the place for eating, giving birth, consummating marriage, receiving visitors, and dying.

Gift Suggestions:

- **A pair of flannel pajamas, a good book, and breakfast in bed**

MOTHERLY LOVE

Give your Mother's Day gift meaning by incorporating a symbolic animal.

CAT
Symbolizes protection, domesticity, fertility

In both ancient Rome and Egypt, the cat was revered as a guardian of the house. The animal symbolized domesticity and fertility.

COW
Symbolizes Mother Earth

Cows are sacred to Hindus and therefore never harmed. They represent Mother Earth, abundance, and fertility. Aditi, a Hindu goddess who is sometimes identified as a cow, is known for her mothering ways.

HIPPOPOTAMUS
Symbolizes fertility, motherhood

In Egyptian mythology, the fertility goddess Taueret had the head of a hippo. Figurines of the goddess were placed near women in childbirth for good luck.

SWALLOW
Symbolizes fertility, motherhood

An Egyptian symbol of motherhood, swallows represent fertility, hope, and fidelity.

TURTLE
Symbolizes fertility, domesticity, strength

Because turtles produce so many eggs, they're seen in many cultures as a symbol of fertility and domesticity. Psychologists see turtles as a symbol of quiet strength, and in Aesop's fable *The Tortoise and the Hare*, the turtle represents determination.

Gift Suggestions:

- A figurine of the animal accompanied by a heartfelt note
- A stuffed animal
- A handmade card featuring the symbolic animal
- A piece of jewelry featuring the animal

- A set of luxurious sheets
- A breakfast-in-bed tray and a cookbook
- A magazine subscription and a bedside reading light
- A set of IOUs to cover Mom's tasks while she stays in bed

FIG
Symbolizes enlightenment, peace, abundance

It was under the fig tree that Siddhartha Gautama (the Buddha) reached enlightenment, and, in the Bible, a fig-bearing tree is a key representation of paradise. If a woman dreams of a basket of figs, it symbolizes her role as goddess or mother.

Gift Suggestions:

- ◁ **A basket of fresh figs or fig jam**
- ◁ **A fig tree**
- ◁ **A fig-scented perfume**
- ◁ **Fig-scented candles, soap, or bath oil**
- ◁ **A dinner made by you featuring figs and other meaningful foods or fruits**

 FLOWERS

Symbolize various meanings

Carnations are the traditional Mother's Day flower in the United States, and in Australia it's chrysanthemums ("Mums for mums!"). But a variety of flowers make meaningful Mother's Day gifts. See Appendix A: The Meaning of Flowers & Trees (pg. 125) for a full list.

 JEWELRY

Symbolizes tradition, honor

In the early 1900s, mothers in France were awarded medals based on how many children they had (perhaps as a way to encourage repopulation after WWI). Mothers with five children were given a bronze medal; six or seven garnered a silver medal; and eight or more children won you a gold medal.

Gift Suggestions:

- ⊰ **A bracelet with the birthstones of her children**
- ⊰ **A charm bracelet with charms representing her children and/or her favorite things**
- ⊰ **A locket or pendant with pictures of family inside**

MOON

Symbolizes home, family

The moon is a feminine symbol that appears in myths as a sister of the sun. It's often associated with home, family, and emotional well-being.

Gift Suggestions:

- ⊰ **A moonlight picnic or beach walk with the whole family**
- ⊰ **A crescent moon pendant**
- ⊰ **A telescope**
- ⊰ **A copy of *The Magical Land of Noom*, by Johnny Gruelle, a classic children's tale about the other side of the moon**

Father's Day

Father's Day wasn't declared a national holiday until 1972, but the idea was conceived decades earlier by a young woman from Spokane, Washington, whose father had raised six kids on his own. Dads can be some of the most challenging people to buy for, and they're frequently given gifts like ties or boxes of cigars year after year. In Japan, however, a woman who gives a man a necktie is said to be "choking" the relationship. So, for a meaningful gift, avoid the traditional tie and keep Dad's hobbies and interests in mind. It'll show how well you know him and how much you care!

BAMBOO

Symbolizes strength, flexibility, longevity, luck, enlightenment

Bamboo can move with the wind but not break, which makes it one of the strongest (and most flexible) building materials. Its evergreen nature is a symbol of longevity, and it's often thought to bring good luck. In Chinese philosophy, the knots on the stalk represent the various steps on the path to enlightenment.

Gift Suggestions:

- ⊰ **A few lucky bamboo stalks in a glass jar**
- ⊰ **A hat, robe, or sheets made from bamboo, one of the softest fibers around**
- ⊰ **Potted bamboo (or a nursery gift certificate) to plant in the backyard**

BOOK

Symbolizes knowledge, wisdom

Books are a bottomless well of knowledge and wisdom and often a symbol of high culture. In a sense, they represent the universe and all it holds.

Gift Suggestions:

- ⊰ **A first edition or signed copy of his favorite book**
- ⊰ **A blank book to record his favorite fatherhood moments**
- ⊰ **A scrapbook celebrating Dad**
- ⊰ **A coffee-table book featuring his favorite hobby**

CEDAR

Symbolizes strength, support, protection, calm

Prized for its strength and its resistance to rot, cedar was used to build Solomon's Temple in Jerusalem. Origen, an early church father, said, "The cedar does not decay. To use cedar for the beams of our house is to protect our soul from corruption." It's used in aromatherapy to ease anxiety and fear.

Gift Suggestions:

- ⊰ **A set of cedar hangers**
- ⊰ **A new sweater or blanket and a cedar sachet to store with it**
- ⊰ **A cedar box or chest for treasures**
- ⊰ **A cedar plank for the home chef, along with a grilling cookbook**

LION

Symbolizes strength, courage, pride, male energy, protection

Known as the king of beasts, the lion symbolizes male energy, courage, strength, and pride. The animal is associated with the sun and often represents protection.

Gift Suggestions:

- ⊰ **A lion adopted in his name from the World Wildlife Fund**
- ⊰ **A lion-themed desk accessory**
- ⊰ **Lion cuff links**

SEA HORSE

Symbolizes good luck, nurturing fathers

A perfect symbol for "Mr. Mom," sea horse males carry and give birth to their young. They're also said to protect fishermen on the Mediterranean.

Gift Suggestions:

- ❧ A copy of Eric Carle's *Mister Seahorse*
- ❧ An aquarium and a few sea horses
- ❧ A sea horse paperweight or figurine

Graduation

Whether the recipients are graduating from grade school or flying the coop for college, gifts for graduation should express independence, maturity, new beginnings, change, and intellect. If the recipient is taking up residence in a dorm or a first apartment, consider packaging something practical (a set of sheets, a coffeepot) with something that symbolizes their transition from one life stage to another. Consult the list below for items that are both practical and meaningful.

AIRPLANE

Symbolizes freedom, independence, aspiration

St. Augustine said, "The world is a book, and those who do not travel read only a page." Airplanes represent an opportunity to explore and experience total freedom and independence. Similarly, flight, especially in dreams, represents achievement of one's dreams, demonstration of personal will, and liberation.

Gift Suggestions:

- ☞ **Plane tickets for a weekend getaway**
- ☞ **Flying lessons**
- ☞ **A model airplane**

⊰ A collection of themed movies, like *Airplane!*, *Planes, Trains and Automobiles*, and *Snakes on a Plane*

AUTOMOBILE
Symbolizes self-control, freedom, responsibility

The car, particularly in America, is the ultimate symbol of freedom. With that freedom, especially as one embarks on adulthood, comes a responsibility to demonstrate self-control.

Gift Suggestions:

⊰ A kit with fancy car wash, wax, a chamois, and interior wipes

⊰ A car ornament or a sterling silver key chain, particularly meaningful for someone receiving her driver's license or moving to a new place

BOOK
Symbolizes knowledge, wisdom

Books are a bottomless well of knowledge and wisdom and often a symbol of high culture. In a sense, they represent the universe and all it holds.

Gift Suggestions:

⊰ A first edition or signed copy of his favorite book

⊰ A blank book to record her own thoughts on this new venture

- A copy of *Oh, the Places You'll Go!*, by Dr. Seuss, with a few words of advice inscribed on the inside
- A subscription to a magazine or newspaper
- A collection of reference books and a set of bookends
- A portfolio or briefcase

COINS
Symbolize wealth, luck, prosperity

In Britain, lucky sixpences are given for many occasions as a wish for good fortune. Silver is also thought to harbor a peaceful energy.

Gift Suggestions:

- A nice jar or container that reflects the recipient's personality, filled with quarters for laundry or parking
- A silver piggy bank and a savings bond or a few shares of stock

COMPASS
Symbolizes direction, balance, spiritual journey

The compass symbolizes direction or finding one's way and makes a great gift for anyone on a journey. In Chinese tradition, the feng shui compass, or Lo P'an, is used to provide deeper meaning about all physical and energetic aspects of a location.

Gift Suggestions

- ⊰ **A compass plus a guidebook to his new college town**
- ⊰ **A compass and a new backpack or piece of luggage**
- ⊰ **A compass and a subscription to a travel magazine**

FROG

Symbolizes change, maturity, good luck

Frogs, who morph from tadpole to full-grown adult, are symbolic of transformation and change. They supposedly have magical powers and are said to bring good luck to travelers.

Gift Suggestions:

- ⊰ **A "nature sounds" sound machine or clock for her dorm room**
- ⊰ **Frog slippers or pajamas**
- ⊰ **A collection of notebooks and other supplies featuring frogs**

HAT

Symbolizes status, responsibility, new beginnings

You can often tell a person's occupation or status just by glancing at his hat (baker, king, graduate), and people who "wear many hats" have numerous responsibilities and jobs. A new hat can welcome a new phase of life and encourage new ways of thinking.

Gift Suggestions:

- ⊰ **A hat from her new school or town**
- ⊰ **Everything she needs to knit her own hat and instructions on how to do so**
- ⊰ **A new hat appropriate for the climate (sun hat, ski hat)**

LIGHTBULB

Symbolizes creativity, spirit, ideas

Generally, light represents the spirit, and lightbulbs are often used in cartoons and pop culture to signify a brilliant idea.

Gift Suggestions:

- ⊰ **A package of energy-saving lightbulbs and a book on going green**
- ⊰ **A lightbulb and a coffee-table book on amazing inventions to spark big ideas**
- ⊰ **An interesting new lamp or reading light**

OWL

Symbolizes wisdom, transformation

A classic symbol of wisdom, owls were used on coins in a number of countries, including Greece, Egypt, Turkey, and Italy. They're sometimes associated with magic and transformation.

Gift Suggestions:

- ⊰ **A luggage tag in the shape of an owl**
- ⊰ **An owl pendant or a pair of earrings**

 PEN

Symbolizes learning, destiny

A symbol of learning, pens represent our ability to make our own way on the page—as well as in life.

Gift Suggestions:

- ⊰ **A monogrammed pen or pen set**
- ⊰ **A beautiful pen with a journal, sketch pad, or stationery**
- ⊰ **A pencil cup or case and a set of personalized pencils**

 PEPPERMINT

Symbolizes concentration

Peppermint is thought to have curative properties and the ability to sharpen the mind and enhance concentration.

Gift Suggestions:

- ⊰ **A "survival package" with peppermint candies and gum, essential oil, lotion, lip balm, and soap**
- ⊰ **A shaving set with mint shaving cream**
- ⊰ **A fun decorative jar filled with peppermint candies for a new room or office**

Retirement

Retirement is one of those events that (typically) only happens once in a lifetime, so it's a great occasion for a meaningful and symbolic gift. The most traditional retirement gift is a gold watch, perhaps because the retiree is likely to have lots of time on his hands. To make a gift like this extra special, package it with something fun to fill that time, like a collection of books, a gift certificate for an art class, a travel guide to somewhere exotic, or a few IOUs from you for dinner or coffee out.

 ## AIRPLANE
Symbolizes freedom, independence, aspiration

St. Augustine said, "The world is a book, and those who do not travel read only a page." Airplanes represent an opportunity to explore and experience total freedom and independence. Similarly, flight, especially in dreams, represents achievement of one's dreams, demonstration of personal will, and liberation.

Gift Suggestions:

- ↲ **A travel guide to somewhere he's been longing to go**
- ↲ **A subscription to a travel magazine**
- ↲ **A coffee-table book on a favorite locale**

BOOK
Symbolizes knowledge, wisdom

Books are a bottomless well of knowledge and wisdom and often a symbol of high culture. In a sense, they represent the universe and all it holds.

Gift Suggestions:

- A book on a favorite hobby or something she'd like to learn
- A first edition or signed copy of her favorite book
- A sketchbook and a set of colored pencils
- A leather-bound journal for recording his thoughts and wisdom

EAGLE
Symbolizes hard work, grace, power, strength

Known as the king of birds, the eagle is a symbol of power and strength. As a Zuni fetish, this majestic bird grants grace through knowledge and hard work, making it an excellent gift for a retiree.

Gift Suggestions:

- An eagle pendant or figurine
- An eagle key chain
- A bird-watching trip to eagle country or an aviary

WATCH
Symbolizes time, transition, new beginnings

Watches are symbolic of the time put into a particular job and of the passing (and preciousness) of time. They remind us that nothing is constant but change and help ring in a new phase of our lives.

Gift Suggestion:

⸎ **A wristwatch or engraved pocket watch**

Bar/Bat Mitzvah

A very special birthday, thirteen is the age of religious responsibility in the Jewish faith, celebrated with a bar or bat mitzvah. The term *bar mitzvah*, however, is a "who" as well as a "what." The words *bar and bat mitzvah* translate to "son and daughter of the commandments." Though traditional Jewish-themed gifts are often given to recognize the special occasion, it's perfectly acceptable to give the same types of gifts that you would for a birthday (so don't forget to peruse that chapter as well!).

 BOOK
Symbolizes knowledge, wisdom

Books are a bottomless well of knowledge and wisdom and often a symbol of high culture. In a sense, they represent the universe and all it holds.

Gift Suggestions:

- **A biography of a Jewish hero or heroine**
- **A subscription to a Jewish magazine**
- **A first edition or signed copy of her favorite book, or a book that was meaningful to you at that age**
- **An album or journal for recording memories of the event**

COINS

Symbolize wealth, luck, peace

In Britain, lucky sixpences are given for many occasions. Silver is also thought to harbor a peaceful energy.

Gift Suggestions:

- A piggy bank, coin purse, or wallet, plus a savings bond to be cashed at a later date
- A few shares of stock from a favorite company
- A high-tech coin sorter with some coins to get started
- An Israeli coin medallion
- Commemorative coins from the birth year and bar/bat mitzvah year

 ## EIGHTEEN

Symbolizes life

In Jewish numerology, the letters that make up the word *chai* or "life" equal eighteen. Wish the recipient "life" by giving a gift that features a multiple of eighteen.

Gift Suggestion:

- Eighteen silver dollars in a special piggy bank

WOOD
Symbolizes life, strength, honor

Wood represents new beginnings and life. In ancient times, Jewish families would plant a tree in honor of the newborn child. The wood from the tree (cedar for boys and cypress or pine for girls) was used for the wedding canopy when the child was ready to marry.

Gift Suggestions:

- ⸜ **A tree planted in Israel in the person's name**
- ⸜ **A special wooden jewelry box or chest to keep treasures**
- ⸜ **A wooden chess set**

APPENDIX A:
THE MEANING OF FLOWERS & TREES

Flowers are a fitting gift for any occasion, and each one harbors historical significance and meaning. You can give the actual flower or tree or a variation, like an essential oil, scented spray, or another meaningful item that features a picture of the flower or tree. You can also easily imbue a gift with symbolism by simply adding a sprig of the fresh flower, a packet of seeds, or an enclosure card featuring the flower.

Flowers

AFRICAN VIOLET	*Peace, spirituality*
AMARYLLIS	*Pride, beauty*
APPLE BLOSSOM	*Promise, temptation*
ASTER	*Love, daintiness, contentment*
AZALEA	*Self-care, womanhood, temperance, ephemeral passion, abundance*
BABY'S BREATH	*Everlasting love, happiness*
BUTTERCUP	*Cheerfulness, childishness*
CACTUS	*Endurance, warmth, bravery*
CAMELLIA	*Admiration, perfection, uniqueness, excellence, steadfastness*

CARNATION (PINK)	*Gratitude*
CARNATION (RED)	*Admiration, pure love*
CARNATION (WHITE)	*Innocence, remembrance, good luck for women*
CHRYSANTHEMUM	*Cheerfulness, friendship, happiness, longevity*
CORNFLOWER	*Delicacy, protection*
CROCUS	*Cheerfulness, youthful gladness, foresight*
DAFFODIL	*Respect, self-love, chivalry, unrequited love*
DAISY	*Innocence, gentleness*
FORGET-ME-NOT	*True love, faithfulness, remembrance*
GARDENIA	*Secret love, joy*
GERANIUM	*Esteem, comfort*
HOLLYHOCK	*Ambition, forgiveness*
IRIS	*Faith, hope, wisdom, inspiration*
JASMINE	*Friendship, love, grace*
LAVENDER	*Devotion, constancy*
LILAC	*Humility, first love, good luck*
LILY	*Beauty, elegance, sweetness*
LILY OF THE VALLEY	*Sweetness, humility*

LOTUS	*Eloquence, truth*
MARIGOLD	*Comfort, sacred affection*
NARCISSUS	*Egotism, formality*
ORCHID	*Love, beauty, refinement, luxury*
PEONY	*Health, prosperity, devotion, healing, happy life and marriage*
POPPY	*Eternal sleep, imagination, consolation*
PRIMROSE	*Youth, hope, young love*
ROSE (PINK)	*Happiness, friendship*
ROSE (RED)	*Passionate love*
ROSE (WHITE)	*Innocence, secrecy*
ROSE (YELLOW)	*Friendship, forgiveness*
SUNFLOWER	*Loyalty, good wishes, pride, ambition*
TULIP	*Fame, charity, love*
VIOLET	*Modesty, innocence, faithfulness, simplicity*

Trees

BAMBOO	*Luck, happiness*
BIRCH	*Meekness, humility*
BLACK POPLAR	*Courage*

CEDAR	*Strength, prosperity*
CHERRY	*Education*
CYPRESS	*Death, mourning*
DOGWOOD	*Durability, charm, finesse*
FIG	*Longevity, fertility, abundance*
MAPLE	*Reserve*
OAK	*Hospitality*
PALM	*Victory*
PINE	*Hope*
WALNUT	*Intellect, protection*
WILLOW	*Loneliness, yearning*

APPENDIX B:

THE MEANING OF GEMSTONES

For years, gemstones have been considered special and magical. Whether you choose the recipient's birthstone or a stone that reflects the occasion and sentiment, gemstones make meaningful gifts that can be kept close to the heart and treasured for years to come.

AMAZONITE	*Success, order*
AMETHYST	*Peace of mind, humility, sobriety, sincerity*
APACHE TEAR	*Protection, good luck*
AQUAMARINE	*Courage, youth, hope, mental alertness*
BLOODSTONE	*Peace, understanding, balance*
CARNELIAN	*Self-confidence, courage, concentration, health*
CAT'S-EYE	*Youth, wealth, mental health*
CORAL	*Wisdom, protection*
DIAMOND	*Invincibility, purity, sincerity*
EMERALD	*Enhanced memory and wits; fertility, faithfulness, good fortune*
GARNET	*Constancy, strength, health, affection, devotion*

JADE	*Purity, immortality, perfection, unconditional love*
LAPIS LAZULI	*Heaven, healing, vision, awareness*
MALACHITE	*Protection, love, luck, loyalty*
MOONSTONE	*Good luck, tenderness, peace*
MOTHER-OF-PEARL	*Fertility, protection (especially of children)*
OBSIDIAN	*Protection, spirituality*
ONYX	*Protection, courage, good fortune*
OPAL	*Fidelity, clarity, faith*
PEARL	*Beauty, perfection*
PERIDOT	*Wealth, mental health, protection*
QUARTZ	*Spirit, intellect*
RUBY	*Royalty, power, protection, heart*
SAPPHIRE	*Heaven, truth, contemplation, good luck, faith, hope, destiny*
TIGEREYE	*Protection, healing, wealth*
TOPAZ	*Fidelity, friendship, trust*
TOURMALINE	*Hope*
TURQUOISE	*Prosperity, protection, healing*

APPENDIX C:
THE MEANING OF COLORS

Color symbolism varies from culture to culture. Here are some of the most common attributes for each color to help you add even more meaning to your gifts.

BLUE	*Tranquillity, reflection, intellect, truth, spirituality*
BROWN	*Earth, humility, simplicity*
GRAY	*Mediation, immortality, security, balance*
GREEN	*Life, youth, luck, hope, growth, renewal*
ORANGE	*Luxury, love, humility, courage*
PINK	*Sensuality, femininity, romance*
PURPLE	*Royalty, pride, justice, clarity of mind*
RED	*Life, energy, passion, good luck, fertility*
WHITE	*Purity, perfection, peace, innocence*

BIBLIOGRAPHY

Becker, Udo. *The Continuum Encyclopedia of Symbols*. New York: Continuum, 1994.

Bennet, Hal Zina. *Zuni Fetishes: Using Native American Objects for Meditation, Reflection, and Insight*. San Francisco: Harper San Francisco, 1993.

Biedermann, Hans. *Dictionary of Symbolism: Cultural Icons and the Meanings Behind Them*. New York: Facts on File, 1992.

Brownstein, Rita Milos. *Jewish Weddings: A Beautiful Guide to Creating the Wedding of Your Dreams*. New York: Simon & Schuster, 2002.

Bruce-Mitford, Miranda. *The Illustrated Book of Signs & Symbols: Thousands of Signs and Symbols from Around the World*. New York: DK Publishing, 1996.

Bryan, Dawn. *The Art and Etiquette of Gift Giving*. New York: Bantam Books, 1987.

Chatham-Baker, Odette. *Baby Lore: Ceremonies, Myths & Traditions to Celebrate a Baby's Birth*. New York: Macmillan Publishing, 1991.

Cirlot, J. E. *A Dictionary of Symbols*. Mineola, NY: Dover Publications, 2002.

Cunningham, Scott. *Cunningham's Encyclopedia of Crystal, Gem, and Metal Magic*. St. Paul, MN: Llewellyn Publications, 1994.

Hageneder, Fred. *The Meaning of Trees: Botany, History, Healing, Lore*. San Francisco: Chronicle Books, 2005.

Mordecai, Carolyn. *You Are Cordially Invited to Weddings: Dating and Love Customs of Cultures Worldwide, Including Royalty*. Phoenix, AZ: Nittany, 1999.

Washington, Deanna. *The Language of Gifts*. Berkeley, CA: Conari Press, 2000.